THE CONFEDERATE HUNDRED

SIX PRESSES! THREE PROPELLED BY STEAM!

ALL OF THEM RUNNING NIGHT AND DAY!

FRANKLIN PRINTING HOUSE

—AND—

BOOK - BINDERY.

GO TO THE

FRANKLIN

PRINTING

HOUSE

WOOD, HANLEITER, RICE & CO.,

Desire to direct public attention to their unequalled facilities for the superior and prompt execution of all work in their line, from

A Small Card to the Largest Volume!

The establishment, in its various departments, is perhaps the most complete in the whole Southern country. It is the object of the proprietors to establish on a permanent basis a SOUTHERN PUBLISHING HOUSE! thereby effectually removing every necessity for sending North to have works issued. Thus far the enterprise has proved highly successful, and the proprietors feel assured that the beneficial results of such an undertaking have yet to be more fully appreciated by our people. The several departments receive the personal supervision of the firm, and satisfaction guaranteed to each and every patron.

THE BOOK–BINDING DEPARTMENT

Is handsomely fitted up with all the modern improvements and conveniences of that branch. Blank-Books ruled and manufactured; Law Works, Medical Works, Music, Magazines, &c., bound in any style desired, and at prices that cannot fail to give satisfaction.

THE JOB PRINTING DEPARTMENT

Is specially complete in every particular; constant additions are being made in the way of such improvements as are introduced into the Typographical world, by which the proprietors are enabled to furnish THE handsomest printing in the Confederated States! Everything, from a Visiting Card to a Mammoth Poster, tastefully executed in any style and color desired. Three of their six Presses are propelled by STEAM, and kept in operation day and night!

Bank Checks,   Bill Heads,
Railroad Blanks,   Professional Cards,
Programmes,   Circulars.
Legal Blanks,   Letter Heads,

And every imaginable variety of Printing promptly attended to at prices but a small advance on New York rates! Printing in

FANCY COLORED INKS,

AND WITH GOLD AND SILVER BRONZES,

IN THE HIGHEST STYLE OF THE ART!

The Proprietors, confident of their ability to give entire satisfaction, solicit a share of public patronage. Orders from all parts of the country will receive their personal attention, and all work promptly forwarded per Express or otherwise, as may be directed.

All letters should be addressed to

WOOD, HANLEITER, RICE & CO.

ATLANTA, GA., 1861.

Advertisement in the Atlanta *Southern Confederacy*.

The Confederate Hundred

A BIBLIOPHILIC SELECTION
OF CONFEDERATE BOOKS

By RICHARD HARWELL

Beta Phi Mu: 1964

Beta Phi Mu Chapbook NUMBER SEVEN

Urbana, Illinois

Library of Congress Catalog Card Number 64-18876

PRINTED BY THE ANTHOENSEN PRESS, PORTLAND, MAINE

PLATES BY MERIDEN GRAVURE CO., CONNECTICUT

THIS BOOK IS FOR

STEVENS, JEAN, AND JONATHAN HILYARD

PREFACE

ALTHOUGH Beta Phi Mu is a society of librarians, its chapbook series until now has published the work of only one member of the profession. That was Lawrence S. Thompson's co-authored *Fine Bindings in America* (No. 2, 1956). Now comes THE CONFEDERATE HUNDRED, written and compiled by one of the profession's most creative bibliologists, Richard Harwell, Librarian of Bowdoin College.

Since the Civil War Centennial began in 1961, Beta Phi Mu's publications committee has examined various proposals for a chapbook which we hoped would be worthy of adding to the vast printed record of that irrepressible conflict. THE CONFEDERATE HUNDRED is our choice.

Mr. Harwell's contributions to the history and bibliography of the American Civil War are too numerous to detail here. Scholars who work in that field know that he has no peer in the art of unearthing lost treasures of Civil War literature for both specialized and general readers. Some future librarian no doubt will assume the pleasant task of compiling and annotating the Harwell Hundred.

As one of the purposes of this series is to foster the art of fine book making, we have encouraged the designer of THE CONFEDERATE HUNDRED to experiment as freely as he desired. Designer for Chapbook No. 7 is Fred Anthoensen who long ago achieved his place as dean of American printers of bibliography. The type is Times Roman in ten and nine point sizes. The text has been printed on Curtis White Colophon paper.

D. A. B.

FOREWORD

A WORK of this sort is not the product of a singly conceived project. It is a by-product of research over many years, carried forward sometimes as part of the day-to-day duties of a working librarian, sometimes as part of special research, sometimes simply as a hobby. It, therefore, is virtually impossible to thank every individual who has helped along the way. Instead, thanks can be sincerely given to the whole freemasonry of librarians and collectors in the knowledge that the same generosity of spirit with which they have given help voids any need of special thanks.

Individual thanks can, and must, be given, however, to Miss Marjorie Lyle Crandall, formerly Assistant Librarian of the Boston Athenæum; Walter Muir Whitehill, Director and Librarian of the Boston Athenæum; Stephen Riley and John Cushing of the Massachusetts Historical Society, Maurice F. Tauber of Columbia University's School of Library Service, James I. Robertson, Jr., Executive Director of the United States Civil War Centennial Commission; George Schwegmann of the Library of Congress, Misses India Thomas and Eleanor Brockenbrough of the Confederate Museum, Richmond; Randolph Church of the Virginia State Library, McDonald Wellford and Dr. Beverley Randolph Wellford of Richmond, John Cook Wyllie of the University of Virginia, Robert H. Woody of Duke University, Lawrence London of the University of North Carolina, Beverly M. DuBose, Jr., of Atlanta; Miss Margaret Jemison of Talladega, Alabama; Miss Llerena Friend of the University of Texas, Austin; Ralph G. Newman of Chicago, George F. Markham, Jr., of Oconomowoc, Wisconsin; David Weber of the Stanford University Library, Miss Mary Isabel Fry and Carey Bliss of the Henry E. Huntington Library, San Marino, California; Everett T. Moore of the University of California, Los Angeles, Library; and Floyd M. Cammack of the University of Hawaii Library. Special thanks of a different sort are due for the encouragement and catalytic influences of Miss Helen Welch of the University of Illinois Library, Miss Alice Appell of the Long Beach, California, Public Library, and Stevens W. Hilyard of the Bowdoin College Library. I am pleased to record my gratitude to the Faculty Research Committee of Bowdoin College for a grant that has speeded the final version of an often revised manuscript and to the Publications Committee of Beta Phi Mu for its consideration of, and work with, THE CONFEDERATE HUNDRED.

The frontispiece is reproduced from a copy of the Atlanta *Southern Confederacy* in the Duke University Library. The circular of J. A. Jones is privately owned. The representations of items 39, 49, 55, 65, 90, and 98 are from copies in the Library of the Boston Anthenæum. The title page of item 34 is reproduced from a copy in the Virginia Historical Society, Richmond. For help in assembling these illustrations I am in scholarly debt to Mr. Whitehill, Mrs. Margaret Hackett, and James E. Belliveau of the Boston Athenæum; to Mrs. Richard W. FitzGerald of Montgomery, Alabama (formerly of the staff of the Duke University Library); and to W. M. E. Rachal of the Virginia Historical Society.

Much of the material in the introduction to the list of books is rewritten from an article "The Cause That Refreshes: Reading, 'Riting, and Rebellion" which appeared in the July 1959 issue of *College and Research Libraries* (XX, 281-88). Other is adapted from previous use by myself in various publications. Some is used here for the first time. I am grateful to Professor T. Harry Williams for permission to quote from his fine article in *The New York Times Book Review* for March 12, 1961. I am most of all grateful to the many Confederate authors who are my sources and my subject for the record they left of life in the Confederate States of America.

RICHARD HARWELL

Bowdoin College
18 *January* 1964

[x]

CONFEDERATE PUBLICATIONS

FOR SALE BY

J. A. JONES,

RALEIGH, N. C.

We have on hand a number of packages containing the following Confederate Publications which we offer to those who are curious to know what could be done in "DIXIE"—unaided by *any other nation*—in the way of Book making, as follows :

The Dixie Primer, by Mrs. M. B. Moore, Price	10
" " Elementary Spelling Book, " "	25
" " First Reader, " "	15
" First Reader for Southern Schools, "	10
Geographical Reader for Dixie Children, "	1.00
Johnson's Common School Arithmetic, "	50
York's English Grammar, "	50
First Book in English Composition, by L Branson, A. M.,	50
Myrtle Leaves—" A Book adapted to the Times," by Rev. A. W. Mangum,	30

The British Partizan—A Tale of Olden Times by a Lady of South Carolina,	50
The Life of Thos. J. Jackson, (Stonewall) by an Ex Cadet,	50
Guide to Claimants of Deceased Soldiers,	25
Songs of Love and Liberty, by a lady of N. C.,	25
The Jack Morgan Songster, by a Captain in Lee's Army,	15
The Southern Zion Songster,	10
The New Testament,	10
Our Own Primary Grammar, by C. W. Smythe,	25
Our Own Elementary Grammar,	25

The foregoing are in packages containing one each, and will be sent to any address on receipt of price.

In addition to the above, we have a few copies each of the following :

School of the Guides, for the use of the Army of the Confederate States, Price,	25
Volunteer's Camp and Field Book, "	50
Napoleon's Maxims of war, "	50
York's Larger Grammar, "	1.00
Bingham's Cæsar, "	1.00
Warren's Surgery, "	1.50
General Orders from the Adjutant Inspector General's Office, C. S. A., from Jan. 1, 1862, to Dec. 31, 1863, inclusive. Price	$2 00
Regulations of the Army of the Conf. States,	2 00
Public Laws of North Carolina, passed by the General Assembly at the Session of 1865 and 66 and 1861 62 63 and 64, together with	

important ordinances *Being a Compend* of the Laws passed in North Carolina during the Rebellion, above 600 pages, 8vo. Law Sheep Price	$400
Primary Geography, (edi. of 1864,) by Mrs M. B. Moore, Price,	3.00

[This is a CONFEDERATE GEOGRAPHY, and has been much sought because of the author's zeal for the "cause." Many copies have been sold for $5 each. The last question and answer is a fair sample of the book. It is as follows :—Q. What is the present drawback to our trade ? A. An unlawful blockade by the miserable and hellish Yankee nation.

Journal of the Convention of the People of North Carolina, held on the 20th day of May, 1861.	3.50

It cannot be said of these books that they are "elegantly printed and bound," or that they are on fine toned, tinted or even *sized* paper. But the reverse CA NBe said with entire safety. Some of them are the most *inelegant* books perhaps ever made. They sell because they show to some extent the feelings of the author in regard to the "situation," the limited resources of the publishers, their inability to procure materials, and the limited knowledge of the workmen in the art of Book-making.

They are prized as mementoes of the "Lost Cause."

☞ Others will be added to the collection as opportunity offer.   Address,

J. A. JONES,

BOOKSELLER, RALEIGH, N. C.

Broadside circular, 1865.

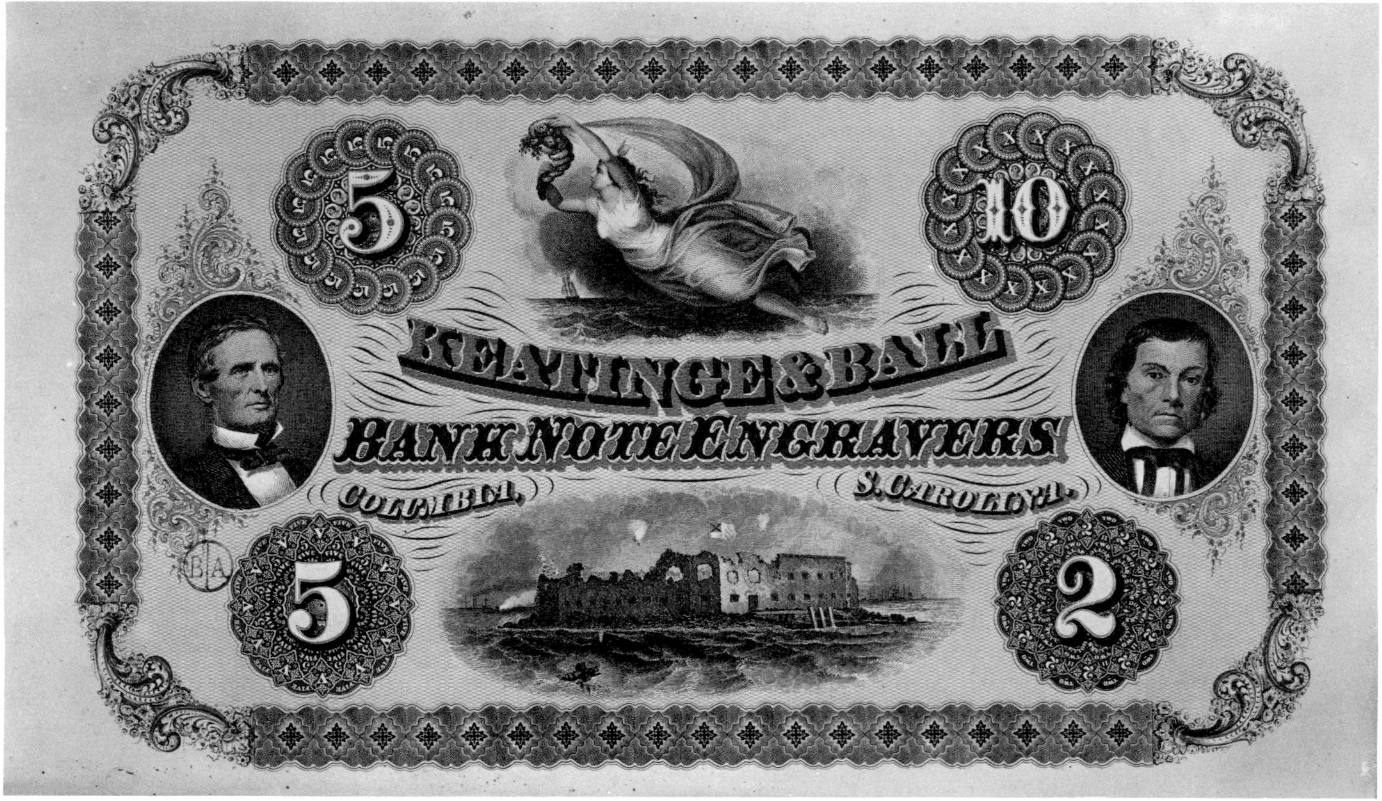

Frontispiece, item 49.

THE CONFEDERATE HUNDRED

HISTORY does not repeat itself. Its seeming repetition is only that the mistakes of one generation are too often repeated by subsequent generations.

There are lessons to be learned from a thorough knowledge of the past: How can we abide the present, how can we face the future, how can we avoid repeating the mistakes of our forebears unless we know what has gone before? In the thorough knowledge of the history of any country there is a suggestion, valid perhaps only as a suggestion, that the past does repeat itself, or hangs on to haunt the present in giving to it a sense of things long gone as part of today. It is this sort of national remembrance that gives us national character. It is this sort of regional remembrance that gives the South regional (sometimes—and too often—sectional) character.

Because knowledge of the past is itself a part of the present, there is in a true understanding of history a sense of timelessness, a sense of immediacy, that links past, present, and future. There is a sense of immediacy, of the present as the durable past, in the words a correspondent for the Chicago *Times* wrote describing the entry of Federal troops into Little Rock, Arkansas in 1863: "An army was never more astonished upon entering a city than ours was upon its entry of Little Rock. Instead of a warm, cordial welcome from the citizens, we were greeted at best with a cold, frigid politeness. . . . A cold, haughty stare met your gaze upon every side, and no sign of genuine welcome was visible anywhere."

Was 1863 very different from 1963?

April 14, 1865 was the fourth anniversary of the fall of Fort Sumter to Confederate forces. Federal officials made that day the occasion of a grand celebration, raising over the ruined fort the same flag which had flown there during Major Robert Anderson's gallant defense of Sumter at the beginning of the Civil War. President Abraham Lincoln was expected to attend, but the press of duties kept him in Washington, and he chose that evening for a fateful visit to Ford's Theater. Anderson, by then a general, did participate in the ceremonies, and the principal address of the occasion was delivered by Henry Ward Beecher, the most famous pastor of that time.

Is it a message of the past, the present or the future that lies in Beecher's words there in Charleston Harbor? "We have shown," he declared, "by all that we have suffered in war how great is our estimate of the importance of the Southern States to this Union, and we will honor that estimate now in peace by still greater exertions for their rebuilding. Will reflecting men not perceive, then, the wisdom of accepting established facts, and with alacrity of enterprise begin to retrieve the past? . . . Since free labor is inevitable, will you have it in its worst forms or its best? Shall it be ignorant, impertinent, indolent, or shall it be educated, self-respecting, moral, and self-supporting? Will you have men as drudges or will you have them as citizens? Since they have vindicated the Government and cemented its foundation stones with their blood, may they not offer the tribute of their support to maintain its laws and its policy? It is better for religion, it is better for political integrity, it is better for industry, it is better for *money*, if you will have that ground motive, that you should educate the black man, and by education make him a citizen. They who refuse education to the black man would turn the South into a vast poorhouse, and labor into a pendulum."

When Beecher spoke at Fort Sumter he spoke only to an audience already sympathetic to his own views. Southerners—ex-Confederates by just a few days—were, quite naturally, not going to turn out to hear a Yankee preacher (especially an abolitionist Yankee preacher, a Black Republican) exult over their defeat. It is, therefore, not inappropriate that Beecher's words be read a century later —when the future of the South, the "importance of the Southern States," still and again hinges on the education of the Negro and full acceptance of Negroes as citizens.

Beecher's words are only one example of the immediacy of history. For bookmen, particularly, there are many others. For the last decade librarians, collectors, and general readers have been again and again reminded of the Civil War by the steady stream of books about it. Not only have librarians, collectors, and thoughtful readers been aware of these books, many have been genuinely alarmed by so many books on a single subject. Such alarm is out of place. The danger is not too many books on one subject but too many bad books on it. The great interest in the Civil War has brought into being its full share of worthwhile history. It has created a public which has made historical research, sometimes at least, lead to immediate financial reward. It has, by the entrance of professional writers into a field that was once the domain of academic historians, made historians learn to write more entertainingly, more effectively. Concomitantly, it has made the hack, journalistic historians write, generally, better histories than the pot-boilers they might have been able to publish a generation ago. T. Harry Williams, a Yankee-turned-Southerner and one of the finest of twentieth-century military historians, summed it up in a 1961 article for *The New York Times Book Review* by quoting Private Carlton McCarthy's *Detailed Minutiae of Soldier Life in the Army of Northern Virginia, 1861-1865:* "But a real good hearty war like that dies hard. No country likes to part with a good earnest war. It likes to talk about the war, write its history, fight its battles over and over again, and build monument after monument to commemorate its glories."

Historian Williams comments:

Popular interest in the war, this "strange sad war," in Whitman's phrase, has always existed. It is possible to check back through any of the scholarly historical quarterlies for the last fifty years or so and find at periodic intervals book reviewers or other critics issuing warnings that run like this (the similarity of the statements is uncanny): "The number of books about the Civil War and Lincoln is reaching a new high. It would seem there is nothing new to be discovered in this period. Obviously the time has come to call a halt."

The halt has never been called, although again we are getting exactly the same kind of warnings, and the scholars have never been able to determine why all this interest in this particular area of our history. The Civil War specialists, it should be noted, always have been and are now as perplexed as anyone else.

Mr. Williams' comments raise two basic questions (in reverse order): Why all this interest in the Civil War; and hasn't the time come to call a halt to writing about it?

Why all this interest? Sir Winston Churchill writes: "The victors forget, the vanquished remember." D. W. Brogan, another distinguished British analyst of America and Americans, calls the Civil War "the most moving, interesting, dignified thing that has ever occurred in America." Mr. Williams emphasizes "the sheer human interest of the war." In the introduction to his *The South to Posterity,*

[xiii]

written nearly a generation ago, Douglas Southall Freeman tried to explain the surge of interest in the Confederacy that welled up after the publication of Margaret Mitchell's *Gone with the Wind* and Clifford Dowdey's *Bugles Blow No More*. "I have to confess," he wrote, "I am not sure I understand all the reasons for the steady increase in the number of those who read deeply of the South's four-year struggle. The reasons must go beyond the familiar emotional appeal of a Jacobite ideal or a 'Lost Cause.' . . . To spirits perplexed or in panic there may be offered in the story of the Confederacy, the strange companionship of misery. In a more positive sense . . . there is stimulation, perhaps inspiration, in making the intimate acquaintance, through candid memoirs of men and women unafraid."

Hasn't the time come to quit writing about it? No. The history of a war belongs, at first at least, to its victors. So it was with our Civil War. Its first relations as history were by Northerners (many of them veterans) who impressed their own interpretations, even their own prejudices, on their accounts. Southerners were slow to answer effectively, for the concentration of editorial and publishing power was at the North. When they did answer, their replies came in a stream of personal apologia and gave to Southern history a stigma of defensiveness. The bitterness left by the war was slow to die, and well into the twentieth century the histories of it were strongly marred by regional or personal prejudices. As a new breed of historians developed in the first quarter of this century they started a gradual reappraisal of the Civil War—this time (with some exceptions) writing history not from a preconception but with honest objectivity. Concomitantly papers which had remained in private hands through the lifetimes of the individuals concerned gradually found their way into public and institutional collections and became the basis for new interpretations and for the development of history into previously unexplored areas. Still with exceptions, this process continues.

Public realization of Civil War history and steadily growing interest in it during the years in which the Civil War Centennial approached did two important things. It made possible the publication of more Civil War books to satisfy the market it created. It also brought to light further records of the war, some as fresh, interesting, and revealing as the accounts long considered classic in this field. To quote Professor Williams once more: "The point here must be made crystal clear. There is always room for a new account that tells us something, and the letters of a private may be as revealing for one dimension of the war as those of a general for another."

Books about the Civil War are published at an amazing rate. Even the excesses of celebration during the centennial years have not killed the interest in the war. There will be periodic fallings off of such interest, and there will be corollary periods of excessive interest; but the Civil War will never lose its very real place as a focal point in American history.

The collecting of Civil War books has grown into a major area of American book collecting along with the intensified growth of interest in the war during the last quarter century. But it is no new thing; Civil War collecting was almost coetaneous with the war itself. The Harvard College Library began the systematic collecting of books about the war in 1861. In a classic statement in the history of the building of American university libraries Librarian John Langdon Sibley wrote in the *Report of the Committee of the Overseers of Harvard College Appointed To Visit the Library for the Year 1861:*

One of the greatest favors to the future historian and philosopher would be to collect all the books, pamphlets, maps, files of newspapers, engravings, photographs, caricatures, ephemeral publications of every kind, even to printed notices, circulars, handbills, posters, letter envelopes, and place them beyond destruction, that as a collection they may reflect the sentiments and feelings, which otherwise will in a great measure pass into oblivion with the occasions which gave them birth. If I could, I would appeal to every inhabitant of the continent to send me everything which could be obtained, in order that every phase of mind, in every section of the country, North, South, East, West, for the Union and against the Union, for secession and against secession, might be represented on our shelves in all the variety of reasoning and imagination, virtue and vice, justice and injustice, fiction and fact, freedom and oppression, kindness and cruelty, truth and caricature, that can be found. I would say, send to me a single pamphlet, book or picture, if you have one to spare.

Similarly, Sidney Root, librarian of the newly formed Baptist Historical Society had written from Atlanta, August 15, 1861 in a letter printed in *The Southern Field and Fireside:*

As part of the current history of the South, it may interest your readers to know that the Baptist denomination of the Confederate States organised, during the last week in July, in our city, an Historical Society. . . .

While the organization has in view the collection and preservation of denomination records, books, statistics, etc., it is also highly desirable to make it the *repertoire* of Southern literature. With this view, contributions to the Library, which is contemplated at this point, are urgently solicited. Bound volumes, or files of newspapers or magazines—pamphlets, maps, manuscripts, pictures, coins, books, etc., are desired, and, if forwarded to the undersigned, will be gratefully acknowledged and properly cared for.

We hope to procure in our Library a copy of every book published in the South. Will Southern authors not give us their assistance?

Would that the wishes of librarians Sibley and Root had been more closely followed! But foresighted preservation of materials in the 1860's did provide the bases for some of the great Civil War collections that now exist. Speaking to a symposium at Bowdoin College in February 1963 Verner Clapp summed it up: "Every old library is, to a degree, a rare book library. After all, the real reason for collecting rare books is that one be able to see as closely as possible what the author actually did say and see it in the form in which he actually said it: This is the way his book appeared; this is what his text read."

"The war is storing up, for the people of the Confederate States," declared Richmond's wartime *Magnolia Weekly*, "the noblest legacies that ever fell to the lot of Nations and Communities." What was true for one side was essentially true for both and was as true of printed materials as of individual or regional traditions. Both North and South could well have heeded the *Magnolia*: "It behooves our people to guard these legacies, that desolating war shall have left them, with jealous care." But jealous care of its printed materials was hardly to the tenor of thinking in the South at the end of the war. Official records in Richmond were carried off to Washington as "captured documents," and the Virginia State Library, as well as private libraries, was looted in the careless irresponsibility characteristic of a conquering army. In the first years of Reconstruction there were more immediate problems than book collecting. Livings had to be made. Book collecting could wait.

The first great Civil War collections grew up in the North. Northern libraries accumulated as part of their normal growth the principal items of Union interest. The greatest of collections of printed materials of the Confederacy had its beginning in purchases Francis Parkman made for the Boston Athenæum when he visited Richmond in the spring of 1865. The documents taken at the fall of Richmond became the basis of the great collection of Confederate materials at the Library of Congress. Appreciation of the abiding value of these records is demonstrated in General Orders, No. 127, of the Adjutant General's Office of the War Department, issued at Washington July 21, 1865:

ORDERED:

That a Bureau be organized in the Adjutant General's Office for the collection, safe-keeping, and publication of the Rebel Archives that have come into possession of this Government, the Bureau to consist of one Chief . . . one assistant . . . and such number of clerks . . . as may be found necessary for the speedy collection of the archives. Doctor FRANCIS LIEBER is hereby appointed Chief of said Bureau, and the Quartermaster General is directed to furnish suitable apartments and buildings for the collation and custody of the archives mentioned.

Collections begun by Union soldiers during the war eventually found their way into libraries and form the core of fine and extensive holdings at Princeton University, the Western Reserve Historical Society, the Newberry Library, the Chicago Historical Society, and Trinity College. Other extensive collections, eminently rewarding for research, in Northern Libraries are at Yale University, Harvard University, the University of Wisconsin, the University of Illinois, and the William L. Clements Library. The Civil War collection of John Page Nicholson, the Lincoln collection of Judd Stewart, and the Confederate collection of Robert Alonzo Brock were brought together to form the great reservoir of materials now a part of the Henry E. Huntington Library. Southerners generally were late joining the game, but there are now fine collections, particularly of Confederate items, at the Confederate Museum, the Virginia Historical Society, the Virginia State Library, the University of Virginia, Duke University, the University of North Carolina, the University of Georgia, Emory University, the University of Alabama, the University of Texas, and Rice University. Each collection has some things unique, some items of special value and interest.

Although Southerners were not soon collectors of Confederate books themselves (with the notable exceptions of Brock and historian Charles Colcock Jones, Jr.) they were quickly aware of the importance of the books, magazines, and newspapers printed during the war as sources to future historians. William R. Smith, a Richmond printer, published in 1865 a broadside offering for sale files of the chief Richmond newspapers and magazines, sets of official Confederate and Virginia publications, and a few miscellaneous pamphlets. Smith's price in 1865 was $100; the same material would now sell (at a conservative estimate) for at least $5,000.

In the same year J. A. Jones, a bookseller in Raleigh, offered a list of twenty-eight miscellaneous items—mostly unofficial publications —for a total of $25 that would a century later command approximately $750. His offer begins: "We have on hand a number of packages containing the following Confederate Publications which we offer to those who are curious to know what could be done in 'Dixie'—unaided by *any other nation*—in the way of Book making. . . ."

As a final note on Jones's broadside he wrote:

It cannot be said of these books that they are "elegantly printed and bound," or that they are on fine toned, tinted or even *sized* paper. But the reverse CAN be said with entire safety. Some of them are the most *inelegant* books perhaps ever made. They sell because they show to some extent the feelings of the author in regard to the "situation," the limited resources of the publishers, their inability to procure materials and the limited knowledge of the workmen in the art of Book-making.

They are prized as mementoes of the "Lost Cause."

A few years later, probably about 1870, William F. Pumphrey, a Richmond book dealer, published as a sales list a *Catalogue of Valuable and Rare Collections of Confederate Miscellany*. His list is headed "rarest of the rare." His items still are. Elusive Confederate publications still delight the collector when they turn up as previously unrecorded items. Though they do not command the high prices of First Folios or even of the finer items of Western Americana, they have a special charm, and to their own inamaratos, an intangible value beyond measure.

The South at war published approximately eight thousand bibliographical items. The exact total will probably never be known, but the bibliographies *Confederate Imprints*, published by the Boston Athenæum in 1955, and *More Confederate Imprints*, published by the Virginia State Library in 1957, are a gratifyingly full record of Confederate publications. These volumes will eventually be supplemented by a record of previously unrecorded items now being compiled by Haskell Monroe of Texas A. & M. College.

The items published in the Confederate South are the expression of every aspect of life in a country at war. Many are of the most minor sort. Many are, verily, "the most inelegant books perhaps ever made." But some are productions impressive for their importance, their quality, or their extent. They form a library to demonstrate the social as well as the military impact of war on a people.

People at war rush into print to vent their emotions. Politicians must explain their positions. Preachers turn out sermons in justification of their points of view. Extremists expound their theories in broadsides and pamphlets. Amateur poets have a field day. It is not remarkable that people in an era of violent feeling should publish extensively; it is a necessity. It is remarkable that the Southern Confederacy devoted so large a proportion of its publishing energy to the non-essentials of day-to-day publishing—to more than a hundred items of belles-lettres, to more than seven hundred sheets of music, to books of travel, to volumes on ancient history.

John R. Thompson, distinguished poet, editor, and State Librarian of Virginia, collaborated with William Gilmore Simms, dean of South Carolina letters in his time, on an anthology of Confederate poetry that was never published. Its introduction (presumably the work of Thompson) is part of the manuscript collections of the Alderman Library of the University of Virginia. It reads in part:

Day by day, the conflict grows more gigantic and more desperate.

But Peace must dawn at last. And when, under its clear light, mankind can individualize the incidents of so momentous a Revolution, they will perceive how varied and important the materials it has furnished to Art.

Dramatist, Song-writer, Painter and Romancist will repair to it as the prolific source whence they shall be tempted to draw both subject and inspiration.

[xix]

Meanwhile, it may be permitted to those whose lot has been cast in the midst of such turbulent events to commemorate in unambitious verse the stirring scenes around them—to chronicle the deeds of patriot soldiers, the devotion of female heroism, the sufferings and the martyrdoms, the elated hopes that wait upon Victory, the stern patience that succumbs not to defeat. And are there any who will censure the authors of this volume, Southern by birth, Southern in principle, feeling and affection, if, sometimes in no measured language, they have expressed their natural scorn of those miscreants in the Army of the North, who, not content with desecrating our hearthstones, would force our Mothers, daughters, sisters, to the level of their brutal and ferocious passions?

Who can weigh his words with the "Proclamation" of a Butler before his eyes, or the groans of McNiell's victims sounding in his ears?

There is little, indeed, in this volume that needs explanation.

If it lacks the genius of the poet, it comes at least from the hearts of men, who, burning with a sense of their country's wrongs, sorrowing in her sorrows, but confident in the vitality of her CAUSE, proud of what has been done by her unaided valour, and under God, serenely sure of her future triumph, have sought to give form in song to their passion.

Thompson (or Thompson and Simms) might as well have been writing an introduction for THE CONFEDERATE HUNDRED. This selection of one collector's choice of the hundred most intriguing, interesting, and important Confederate books rings as fully with the emotions of the wartime South as do the topical poems being presented by Thompson and Simms. The whole scope of the literature of a people is reflected in these hundred books and, as truly as does poetry, indicates what Simms in his introduction to a postwar anthology called "the true *animus* of the action."

When during the war William M. Burwell wrote for Richmond's magazine *The Age* a flowery opening address he was trying to impress on his fellow Confederates the necessity of presenting to the world a literature which would fairly represent their history. "The history of the world," he said, "is the history of Literature in its many forms. The Author, next to Fact, is the great creator of events. The earth, under his magical touch, becomes astir with heroes, and battles, and dynasties. Brass and marble may pass away, adamant may crumble into indistinguishable dust, races of men fall before other and new races of men in the wonderful economy of Nature; but those peoples and events and cities that have been delineated in the writings of the Author can laugh to scorn old Time, for he can no longer say to them: Come, you are mine—pass away with me!"

This then is THE CONFEDERATE HUNDRED: a bit of history (and of literature in its widest and realest sense), a representation of the life of a beleaguered nation during the fifty-two months of its existence. Not because of its books, but because of a heroic people who made the events the books record, the Confederacy lives in history and in the affections of its real and spiritual descendants to a degree out of proportion to its span of existence. For the Confederacy embodied much to endear it to future generations: the position of the underdog and, finally, the romance of a lost cause, the daring of gallant soldiers, the personal attraction of a magnificent military hero. THE CONFEDERATE HUNDRED embodies much of the Confederacy, for in the printed pages the Confederates wrote and read, the Confederacy they knew still lives.

The list is an effort to represent fairly the whole range of Confederate books through a careful sampling of them. The brevity of listings in bibliographies totalling thousands of items does not permit the inclusion of the details which make the study of Confederate imprints such a fascinating avocation. The reduction of the list of Confederate books to a selection of a hundred titles with full publication notes and selected comments—*from the books themselves or from contemporary reviews of them; always only from sources that could have been available to a Confederate reader*—gives the volumes a chance to speak for themselves and to carry to twentieth-century readers something of the spirit they brought to Confederate readers.

What were the criteria for admission to the list? None but the personal taste of the compiler as it has developed over a quarter of a century of working closely with Confederate books. To phrase it differently, the compiler put together THE CONFEDERATE HUNDRED in response to his own imagined question: "If you could own a hundred Confederate books—only a hundred, but any hundred— which would you choose?" The answer has been a full decade in the making, with many changes from the first, tentative selections. Through all the changes the basic purpose has remained to represent the Confederacy through titles that would give an inclusive picture of Confederate printing and literature—a picture sometimes important, sometimes homely, sometimes realistic or critical, sometimes political, sometimes literary, and always a representation of the real Confederacy.

As it was first compiled the selections included a somewhat wider geographical representation of wartime publishing in the South as at least one document from each of the Confederate state governments was present. And there was a larger selection from the very important area of official documents of the Confederate government. But too many intriguing unofficial publications still demanded a place on the list. One by one official titles gave way to other publications till, finally, the state governments are represented only by two key documents from the Secession Convention of South Carolina and the Confederate government by less than a dozen of the nearly two thousand publications it issued.

Other titles in the original list also fell by the wayside: John Fentonhill's *Joan of Arc* (Richmond: 1864), a generally mature thesis but one marred by the author's strained interpolation into French history of a Confederate parallel and by his over-zealous advocacy of raising the Black Flag against the Yankees; Hiram Fuller's *The Times: or, The Flag of Truce* (Richmond: 1863) an intriguing political statement; Charles Colcock Jones, Jr.'s *Monumental Remains of Georgia* (Savannah: 1861), a scholarly treatment of Indian antiquities; Benjamin Morgan Palmer's *The Oath of Allegiance* (Richmond: 1863), an important tract by an important Presbyterian clergyman; William Henry Peck's *The Conspirators of New Orleans* (Greenville, Ga.: [c. 1863]), a novel of the Battle of New Orleans and an excessively rare, early production of a forgotten, but incredibly successful, American sensation monger; Charles Todd Quintard's *The Confederate Soldier's Pocket Manual of Devotion* (Charleston: 1863)—in favor of his more appealing *Balm for the Weary and the Wounded*; William Spottswood White's biography of his son, *Sketches of the Life of Captain Hugh A. White of the Stonewall Brigade* (Columbia: 1864); and E. A. Pollard's *The Seven Days' Battle in Front of Richmond* (Richmond: 1862)—because even this prolific and contemporaneously important Confederate historian could not be represented too many times.

It was determined in the beginning that THE CONFEDERATE HUNDRED must be limited to books and pamphlets. Newspapers and magazines must be omitted. Maps, sheet music, and broadsides would have to be left out. Many publications in these categories have their own importance, their own romance, their own special attraction, but, for the list to be meaningful, this could not be the place for them.

More to the point than the omissions are the inclusions in the list. Here is a wide range of Confederate publications—a sampling of typical and interesting items from many facets of Confederate life. Here is THE CONFEDERATE HUNDRED.

Let its books now speak for themselves.

THE CONFEDERATE HUNDRED

THE CONFEDERATE HUNDRED

ABRAMS, ALEXANDER SAINT CLAIR   1

A full and detailed history of the siege of Vicksburg, by A. S.
Abrams . . . Atlanta, Georgia: Intelligencer Steam Power Presses,
1863.
80 p. 21.5 cm.

"The author claims the right of knowing as much about the siege of
Vicksburg as anyone residing in that town, from the fact that he was at
that point, in Company A, Withers' Light Artillery, as a private, when the
first gun was fired in its defense, and served as such until the raising of the
first siege. In September, 1862, he was discharged from the army on account of sickness, and being unable to return to his home, (New Orleans)
obtained a position in the office of the 'Vicksburg Whig,' where he remained until its destruction by fire in the early part of May, 1863, and
was taken prisoner and paroled after the surrender."—"Author's preface," p. 4.
Entered for copyright in the District Court of the Northern District of
Georgia November 11, 1863.
Crandall 2612.*

AUGUSTA, GEORGIA. Saint Paul's Church   2

Funeral services at the burial of the Right Rev. Leonidas
Polk, D.D., together with the sermon delivered in St Paul's
Church, Augusta, Ga., on June 29, 1864: being the feast of St.
Peter the Apostle . . . Columbia, S. C.: Printed by Evans & Cogs-
well, 1864.
28 p.

Biblical quotation in title.
The funeral address was delivered by Bishop Stephen Elliott.
Crandall 2559.

* Crandall numbers refer to Boston Athenæum, *Confederate Imprints: A Check
List Based Principally on the Collection of the Boston Athenæum*, by Marjorie Lyle
Crandall, with an introduction by Walter Muir Whitehill ([Boston:] The Boston
Athenæum, 1955), 2 v. Harwell numbers refer to Richard Harwell, *More Confed-
erate Imprints* (Richmond, Va.: The Virginia State Library, 1957), 2 v.

[3]

The letters of Mozis Addums to Billy Ivvins. Richmond: West & Johnston, 1862.

1 p. l., 87 p. 20.5 cm.

Cover-title omits imprint.

"To the Bois In the Ommy. | Deare Fellers: | Mr. Weston Jonsum have kinely printed my Letters in a Booke, fer you beenyfit manely. I wisht it cood have apeared while you all wuz in winter qortuz—it mighter wiled away a tejus our or 2. But heer it is ennyhow—better late than nuvver; and here's a hoapinge it may give you a harty laff or too and drive dull keer away a short distunce."—"Pree-Fase," p. [3].

"This is an admirably humorous production from the genial pen of the genial editor of the Literary Messenger."—West & Johnston, *Descriptive Catalogue of Publications* ([Richmond: 1864]), p. 21.

Crandall 3118.

BARDE, ALEXANDRE, 1811?-1863   4

Histoire des comités de vigilance aux Attakapas, par Alexandre Barde . . . Saint-Jean-Baptiste (Louisiane): Imprimerie du Meschacébé et de l'Avant-Coureur, 1861.

2 p. l., vi, [7]-428 p. 17.5 cm.

Quotation in title.
Introduction by Eugène Dumez.
Crandall 2614.

THE BATTLE OF FORT SUMTER and first victory of the Southern troops, April 13th, 1861. Full account of the bombardment, with sketches of the scenes, incidents, etc. Compiled chiefly from the detailed reports of the Charleston press. Published by request. Charleston: Steam-power Presses of Evans & Cogswell, 1861.   5
35 p. front. (fold. map). 23 cm.

The folding map (of Charleston harbor) "cut expressly for the Mercury, F. W. Bornemann, Cha. S. C."
Cover-title adds engraving of Palmetto flag with accompanying motto: *"Animus opibusque parati;"* and: "Price, twenty-five cents."
Crandall 2616.
Issued also in an edition of 32 pages (Crandall 2615).

Slavery and abolitionism, as viewed by a Georgia slave. By Harrison Berry, the property of S. W. Price, Covington, Georgia. Atlanta, Georgia: M. Lynch & Co., Publishers. Printed at the Crusader Office, 1861.

3 p. l., [v]-vi, 46 p. front. (port.). 21.5 cm.

Cover-title adds: "Price 25 cents a copy."

"In offering this address to the public, I do it with the most profound humility, knowing it to be a task worthy of a better-learned and more intelligent writer than myself. But when it is taken into consideration, the cause by which I was actuated may be an excuse for my presumption; for I am a Slave, and have been all my life, and therefore, claim the opportunity, at least, of knowing what Slavery is, and what it is not. And in showing the effect the agitation of Slavery has upon the Slaves generally, I have endeavored to keep within the boundaries of moderation, unless forced by undoubted facts to depart therefrom. In speaking of the citizens of the Northern States, I have in a great many places, summed them all up together; but my intention is to cast no reflections, whatever, upon the conservative citizens of that section. My address is to the fanatical Abolitionists, who call themselves Republicans. To them, and them alone, have I written."—"Preface," p. [v].

"I will not merely say that I *think* he wrote it, for I can safely say I know him to be the author—the sentiments are his, for I have heard him express them time and again, long before I ever dreamed of his writing a book. . . .

"His pamphlet is published by himself, copy-righted for his benefit, and the profits from its sale, should any arise, will be his. I cheerfully commend it to the public, believing that it should be generally patronized. The time he has devoted to writing his book, is generally occupied by other Slaves in making their pocket change. A. M. EDDLEMAN. Atlanta, Georgia, February 26, 1861."—"To the Public," p. viii.

Crandall 2883.

Another edition published by Franklin Printing House: Wood, Hanleiter, Rice & Co., Atlanta, Ga., 1861. 41 p. 21.5 cm. (Crandall 2882).

BUCHANAN, W. JEFFERSON 7

Maryland's hope: her trials and interests in connexion with the war. By W. Jefferson Buchanan . . . Richmond: West & Johnston, 1864.

62 p. 23 cm.

"The final success of the Confederate cause, securing, as it inevitably will, the lasting existence on this continent of the great principle of State's Rights, must consequently preserve to the uttermost bounds the territorial integrity of the entire South. Virginia all, to the very extreme of the 'pan handle;' Maryland all, to her remotest edge; the invaded territory of all the South will yet be re-ransomed, reclaimed from a despotic thraldom by the valor of Southern arms under the genius of the principle of State's Rights. This is the country's belief—and it is Maryland's hope."—p. 60.

"In a previous pamphlet, entitled 'Maryland's Crisis,' to which 'Maryland's Hope' is a sequel, he presented with great force the various disadvantages of the present position of his State, and the difficulties confronting her union with the South. In the pamphlet before us he views the bright side of the picture, and with much earnestness and ability urges the importance and necessity of a future political connexion between Maryland and the Confederate States."—*Southern Literary Messenger,* XXXVI (1864), 127.

Crandall 2701.

BURROWS, JOHN LANSING 8

The New Richmond Theatre. A discourse, delivered on Sunday, February 8, 1863, in the First Baptist Church, Richmond, Va. By J. L. Burrows, D.D., pastor. Richmond: Smith, Bailey & Co., 1863.
Cover-title, 16 p. 21 cm.

"To-morrow night the New Richmond Theatre is to be opened. I deem it fitting, in addition to the notices so liberally given through the daily press, to give this public notice from the pulpit. With surprising energy, and regardless of cost, in these pinching times of war, a splendid building, with most costly decorations, has been reared from the ashes of the old. ... The work is completed; the decorations are finished, and to-morrow night the New Richmond Theatre is to be opened. A strong corps of actors, male and female, have been secured, and, in addition to them, *'twenty gentlemen* for the chorus and the ballet.' No cripples from the battlefields are these—they can sing and dance; they can mimic fighting on the stage. For the serious work of repelling a real enemy they have neither taste nor heart. But they can sing while the country groans, and dance while the cars are bringing, in sad funeral procession, the dead to their very doors, and the dismal ambulance bears the sick and wounded under the very glare of their lights, and within the sound of their music. They keep themselves out of the war for the noble duty of amusing the populace. Should they not, in these times, be especially encouraged, particularly by those whose own brave sons are in the camp or in the hospital, or whose mangled bodies are mouldering in uncoffined graves? Does it not seem a peculiarly happy time for theatrical amusements? Shall we all go and laugh and clap to the music and the dance, while the grasp of relentless foes is tightening upon the throats of our sons, and the armed heels of trampling hosts are bruising the bosom of our beloved mother land?"—p. ₍3₎.

Crandall 4130.

CANTRELL, OSCAR ALEXANDER   9

Sketches of the first regiment Ga. Vols. Together with the history of the 56th Regiment Georgia Vols., to January 1, 1864. By Lieutenant Oscar A. Cantrell. Atlanta, Georgia: Intelligencer Steam Power Presses, 1864.

iv, ₍5₎-73 p. 23 cm.

"We do not find a full and complete record of important and interesting events, such as might appear were the Author an historian, but we find events recorded of minor importance, which, in many places, is done to show the manner in which the soldier passes his life."—"Preface," p. ₍iii₎.

Crandall 2617.

CHISOLM, JOHN JULIAN, 1830-1903   10

A manual of military surgery, for the use of surgeons in the Confederate Army; with an appendix of the rules and regulations of the Medical Department of the Confederate Army. By J. Julian Chisolm . . . Third edition, carefully revised and improved. Columbia: Evans and Cogswell, 1864.

xxiii, 529, ₍26₎ p. 26 plates on 13 ll. 18.5 cm.

" 'Probably the most valuable portion of the Work is contained in the first four chapters, which relate to the hygieina of troops on the march and in camp—the organization and management of hospitals—the duties of the surgeon in camp and on the field of battle, &c. In the remaining chapters will be found a very full and excellent account of the treatment of gun-shot and other wounds and injuries, and their various complications, constituting an admirable guide to the Military Surgeon in most of the emergencies which he may be called upon to encounter. The Regulations of the Medical Department contained in the Appendix, are of course a *sine qua non* to every Medical Officer.'—*Professor Joynes, Virginia Medical College.*"—West & Johnston, *Descriptive Catalogue of Publications* (ₜRichmond, 1864ₜ), p. 9.

Crandall 3029.

First edition, Charleston: Evans & Cogswell, 1861. xi, 447 p. (Crandall 3026). An issue with the same date and paging published in Richmond by West & Johnston (Crandall 3027). Second edition: Richmond: West & Johnston, 1862. xii, 514 p. (Crandall 3028).

CLARKE, H. C.   11

Diary of the war for separation, a daily chronicle of the principal events and history of the present revolution, to which is ₜ*sic*ₜ added notes and descriptions of all the great battles, including Walker's narrative of the battle of Shiloh. By H. C. Clarke . . . ₜVicksburg: H. C. Clarke, c. 1862ₜ.

191 p. 22 cm.

Printed at Augusta, Georgia, Steam Press of Chronicle and Sentinel. "Diary of the war" continues through January 2, 1863.

Crandall 2618.

Another edition: Vicksburg: Clarke's Southern Publishing House, 1862. 56 p. (Crandall 2619).

CONFEDERATE RECEIPT BOOK, a compilation of over one hundred receipts, adapted to the times. Richmond, Va.: West & Johnston, G. W. Gary, Printer, 1863.   12

28, ₜ1ₜ p. 21 cm.

"The accompanying receipts have been compiled and published, with a view to present to the public in a form capable of preservation and easy reference many valuable receipts which have appeared in the Southern newspapers since the commencement of the war. With these have been incorporated receipts and hints derived from other sources, all designed to supply useful and economical directions and suggestions in cookery, housewifery, &c., and for the camp."—"Advertisement," p. ₜ3ₜ.

Crandall 2906.

CONFEDERATE STATES OF AMERICA. Congress   13

Address of Congress to the people of the Confederate States . . . ₜRichmond: 1864ₜ.

8 p. 23 cm.   [8]

Caption title.

The *Address* is believed to have been written by J. L. M. Curry.

"Resolved by the Congress of the Confederate States, That the present is deemed a fitting occasion to remind the people . . . they are engaged in a struggle for the preservation both of liberty and civilization; and that no sacrifice of life or fortune can be too costly which may be requisite to secure to themselves and their posterity the enjoyment of these inappreciable blessings; and also to assure them that, in the judgement of the Congress, the resources of the country, if developed with energy, husbanded with care, and applied with fidelity, are more than sufficient to support the most protracted war which it can be necessary to wage for our independence . . ."—"Joint Resolution in Relation to the War," p. ₍1₎.

Crandall 73.

Another edition has title *Address of the Confederate Congress to the people of the Confederate States.* 16 p. 23 cm. "Mr. Hunter's farewell address to the Senate," p. 15-16 (Crandall 74).

CONFEDERATE STATES OF AMERICA. Congress   14

. . . Proceedings of the Congress on the announcement of the death of Col. Francis S. Bartow, of the Army of the Confederate States, and late a delegate in the Congress, from the State of Georgia. Published by order of the Congress, by J. J. Hooper, secretary. Richmond: Enquirer Book and Job Press: Tyler, Wise & Allegre, 1861.

29 p. 16.5 cm.

At head of title: Congress of the Confederate States.

"3,500 copies . . . to be printed for the use of Congress."—"Resolution of the Congress," July 25, 1861, p. ₍3₎.

Crandall 77.

CONFEDERATE STATES OF AMERICA. Constitution   15

Constitution of the Confederate States of America, adopted unanimously by the Congress of the Confederate States of America, March 11, 1861. Montgomery, Ala.: Shorter & Reid, Printers, Advertiser Office, 1861.

22 p. 21.5 cm.

"The Constitution of the Southern Confederation . . . differs from that of the old Union mainly in the following points. The Southern Constitution absolutely prohibits the over-sea slave trade; that of the Union does not. It permits cabinet members to take part in the discussions of Congress. It prohibits bounties or duties to foster any branch of industry. After a specified time the post-office must cover its own expenses. Log-rolling is prohibited. The President to hold office for six years, and is not to be re-eligible. The subordinate government officers not to be removed by the President without a report to the Senate giving his reasons."—James Spence, *The American Union* (Richmond: 1863), p. 220.

Crandall 1.

Published in numerous other editions (Crandall 2-14).

CONFEDERATE STATES OF AMERICA. Laws, statutes, etc.   16

. . . The statutes at large of the provisional government of the Con-federate States of America, from the institution of the govern-ment, February 8, 1861, to its termination, February 18, 1862, inclusive. Arranged in chronological order. Together with the Constitution of the provisional government, and the permanent Constitution of the Confederate States, and the treaties concluded by the Confederate States with Indian tribes. Edited by James M. Matthews, attorney at law, and law clerk in the Department of Justice. Richmond: R. M. Smith, Printer to Congress, 1864.
xv, [1], 411, xlviii p. 24 cm.

At head of title: By authority of Congress.

"Mr. Matthews's labors in preparing his well known Digests of the Civil and Criminal Code of the Commonwealth of Virginia, fitted him for the performance of his duties in the distinguished position he now holds. The work before us bears evidence of his pains-taking industry, his skill, taste and method. The laws are admirably arranged, with copious marginal notes and an excellent index. The book is well printed on good paper."—*Southern Literary Messenger,* XXXVI (1864), 64.

Crandall 19.

Continued as: The statutes at large of the Confederate States of America (Richmond: 1862-64), 5 v. (paged continuously, with separate title pages for *Public laws* and *Private laws*) (Crandall 20-24).

CONFEDERATE STATES OF AMERICA. Navy department   17

[Report of Flag Officer Buchanan. Richmond: 1862].
13 p. 21 cm.

"Message of the President . . . April 10, 1862 . . . transmit,ting, to Congress a communication from the Secretary of the Navy, covering a 'detailed report of Flag Officer Buchanan, of the brilliant triumph of his squadron over the vastly superior forces of the enemy, in Hampton Roads, on the 8th and 9th of March last.'"
Crandall 874.

CONFEDERATE STATES OF AMERICA. President (Jefferson Davis) 18

Inaugural address of President Davis, delivered at the Capitol, Monday, February 18, 1861, at 1 o'clock, p.m. Montgomery, Ala.: Shorter & Reid, Printers, 1861.
8 p. 23.5 cm.

"Sustained by the consciousness that the transition from the former Union to the present Confederacy has not proceeded from a disregard on our part of just obligations, or any failure to perform any constitutional duty—moved by no interest or passion to invade the rights of others—anxious to cultivate peace and commerce with all nations, if we may not hope to avoid war, we may at least expect that posterity will acquit us of having needlessly engaged in it. Doubly justified by the absence of wrong on our part, and by wanton aggression on the part of others, there can be no cause to doubt that the courage and patriotism of the people of the Confederate States will be found equal to any measure of defence which honor and security may require."—p. 4-5.
Crandall 607.

CONFEDERATE STATES OF AMERICA. War department 19

General orders from Adjutant and Inspector-General's office, Confederate States Army, from January, 1862, to December, 1863 (both inclusive). In two series. Prepared from files of head-quarters, Department of S. C., Ga., and Fla. With full indexes. Columbia: Presses of Evans & Cogswell, 1864.
2 v. in 1 (xlvii, 159; lix, 276 p.). 18.5 cm.

Includes certain General orders, January to March, 1864, v. 2, p. 243-76.
"The work is very handsomely executed, and we recommend it to the public and to the officers of the army especially, as a most valuable pub-lication."—*Southern Literary Messenger,* xxxvi (1864), 318.

Each General order was also issued as a separate item.
Crandall 1343.

Continued by the same publishers with volumes "from January 1, 1864, to July 1, 1864, inclusive" (1864) and "from July 1, 1864 to December 31, 1864" (1865). Preceded by publication of the General orders for 1862 as a separate volume (1863). (Crandall 1344, 1345, 1346, 1342.)

CONFEDERATE STATES OF AMERICA. War department   20
Reports of the operations of the Army of Northern Virginia, from June 1862, to and including the battle of Fredericksburg, Dec. 18, 1862 . . . Richmond: R. M. Smith, Public Printer, 1864.
2 v. 22 cm.
Crandall 1435.

CONFEDERATE STATES OF AMERICA. War department   21
Uniform and dress of the Army of the Confederate States . . . Richmond: Chas. H. Wynne, printer, 1861 [i. e. 1862].
5 p. 15 plates (8 col.) 35.5 x 28 cm.

Published by Blanton Duncan.
In imprint: Lithography by E[r]nest[1] Crehen.
Color printing by J. T. Wagner, Nashville.
Lithographic printing of uncolored plates by P. L. Valory, Petersburg.
Tipped in are a copy of General orders, No. 4, Adjutant and Inspector General's office, January 24, 1862, marking additions to the uniform regulations and a strip illustrating the various forage caps.
Crandall 1450.

This edition was preceded by another with only black and white plates (Crandall 1449).

"A limited edition. Only 1,000 copies of this work, the authorized standard, will be shortly issued.

"The distinction between the various grades are shown by the plates, of which there will be fifteen, and consisting of all the different departments of the service, and comprising about fifty figures. This edition will be plain black, and will be followed by another edition in full colors—a magnificent work. It contains plates, and also full direction for the guidance of tailors."—Advertisement of Col. Blanton Duncan, Richmond, Virginia, in the Atlanta *Southern Confederacy*, September 1, 1861.

Address to Christians throughout the world. ₍Richmond: 1863₎. 12 p. 24.5 cm.

Caption title.

"In publishing the foregoing address it is proper to declare explicitly, that its origin was from no political source whatever, but from a conference of ministers of the gospel in the city of Richmond.

"The signatures are confined to this class because it was believed that, on the points presented, the testimony of men holding this office might be received with less prejudice than that of any other. These signatures might have been indefinitely increased. Only a limited number of names —much less than at first intended—was solicited; and as they are still coming in, some will probably be received too late for insertion. Those appended represent more or less fully every accessible section of the Confederacy, and nearly every denomination of christians ₍*sic*₎. They are ample for the chief object intended, namely, to bear witness to the christian world that the representations here made concerning the public sentiment of the South are true, and to carry a solemn protest against the continuance of this fruitless and unrighteous war."—"*Notes*," p. 12.

"If we were moved to make this address by any fears of the final issue of the war in which our country is now engaged, by any inclination to meddle with political questions, by any desire to resume controversy in respect to matters which have been referred to the arbitration of the sword; if indeed anything that compromised the simplicity, dignity and purity of christian duty moved us to issue this address, we should deserve to have it despised by you, and could hope for no blessing of God to rest upon it. But for all that we say in the following declarations, we are willing to be judged by succeeding generations, and to answer in that day when the secrets of all hearts shall be made known."—p. ₍1₎.

Signed by ninety-six Protestant churchmen.

Crandall 4269.

Published in Philadelphia (1863) as *An address to Christians throughout the world*. By a convention of ministers, assembled at Richmond, Va., April, 1863. 20 p., 1 l. 22 cm.

Published in London (1863) as *Address to Christians throughout the world*. By the clergy of the Confederate States of America. 16 p. 22 cm. Printed by Strangeways and Walden.

The life of Stonewall Jackson. From official papers, cotemporary narratives and personal acquaintance. By a Virginian . . . Richmond: Ayres & Wade, Illustrated News Steam Presses, 1863. xi, [1], [13]-305 p. front. (port.). 19 cm.

Quotation in title.

Frontispiece is a lithograph by Ernest Crehen of a photograph of Jackson taken by D. T. Cowell; the portrait on the cover is a woodcut by Hurdle.

"This work has been written under disadvantages which entitle it to the liberal criticism of the reader. It was undertaken without thought of the probable activity of the summer campaign, and has been composed in bivouac—by the road-side—immediately before and after engagements —amid scenes and under circumstances which have rendered deliberate writing impossible. This, and my inability to correct the proof-sheets, should excuse the errors of the work.

"All that I claim for the narrative is *truth*. This I think it possesses, and the merit is not trifling. Beyond its value as an accurate statement of events, derived in the main from official documents, I claim nothing for it—style least of all."—"To the reader," p. [iii].

" 'It not only gives an interesting and faithful sketch of Jackson's life, but abounds in personal incidents and anecdotes illustrating the glorious character of the deceased, and is in itself an admirable history of the war.'—*Richmond Dispatch*."—West & Johnston, *Descriptive Catalogue of Publications* ([Richmond: 1864]), p. 21.

"We had determined, four months before the death of General Jackson, to publish his memoirs in popular form. . . . The death of General Jackson neither advanced or delayed the publication an hour. . . .

"We entrusted the materials which we had collected to Major John Esten Cooke. We selected Mr. Cooke for a variety of reasons. He stood high in the literary world. He had already been the author of many works. He was a man of irreproachable character, and had led a laborious life from his boyhood. Holding a position upon the staff of Gen. Jeb. Stuart, he was enabled to watch and carefully study the movements of Gen. Jackson. This last circumstance we thought a matter of considerable importance. Everybody can tell, in the twinkling of an eye, the vast difference between the narrative of a person who has seen what he describes, and that of a person who obtains his knowledge at second hand. Major Cooke, moreover, is a master of a lively style, excels in description, and was in every way the proper person to produce a lively, popular history of the great warrior."—Statement of Ayres & Wade, *The Southern Illustrated News*, II (1863), 34.

Crandall 2563.

THE COTTON FIELD MELODIES. Augusta, Ga.: Published by Blackmar & Bro., c. 1833 [i. e. 1863].   24
Cover-title, 36 p. 14 cm.

A collection of the words of thirty-five popular songs.

Includes: "Catalogue of sheet music published and for sale by Blackmar & Bro., Augusta, Ga."

Entered for copyright in the District Court of the Southern District of Georgia May 27, 1863.

Harwell 1275.

CROSS, JOSEPH, 1813-1893   25
Camp and field: papers from the portfolio of an army chaplain. By Rev. Jos. Cross, D.D. Macon, Ga.: Burke, Boykin & Company, 1864.
4 v. in 3. Vols. I and II: 17.5 cm.; vol. III & IV: 18 cm.

Cover-title of vols. I and II: Camp and field. In four books: I. Diorama of 1862. II. New dispensation. III. Outlook from Torytown. IV. Gallery of portraits. "Book second" added to title page of vol. II. "Books third and fourth" added to title page of combined volume. The final volume has imprint: Columbia, S. C.: Printed by Evans & Cogswell, 1864.

"On the fourth of July, 1861, the author of these PAPERS entered the Confederate service as Chaplain of the Second Regiment of Tennessee Volunteers, commanded by Colonel—now Major General—WILLIAM B. BATE.

"Six months in camp and field on the lower Potomac furnished abundant material for a book. I returned to Nashville to put it to press. The publishers, in consideration of five hundred dollars paid in advance, commenced the work with the most commendable zeal. Early in February, 1862, the stereotype plates were finished, and the last proof-sheets revised. The author hastened to rejoin the army in Virginia. In three weeks, at most, the book was to follow him.

"Alas! there is nothing certain but human uncertainty. Fort Donelson fell, and with it fell THE BANNER OF THE REGIMENT.

[15]

"Messrs. Johnson, Rosecrans & Co., now have possession of the stereotype plates, with the entire material and apparatus of publication. It is plausibly whispered and earnestly hoped, that they intend to issue the volume at an early day, for the illumination and edification of the subjects and soldiers of Abraham The First. The author would suggest for their consideration—very humbly, however, and with great deference to their superior judgment—a long and elaborate introduction by the Rev. Henry Ward Beecher, copious and very erudite foot-notes by the Hon. Charles A. Sumner, and numerous artistic illustrations in the highest style of the engraver, not ommitting Great Bethel, Bull Run, and Leesburg—as likely to add no little to the interest of the work and the profits of its sale.

"Meanwhile, he begs leave to resume the narrative, interspersing biographical and characteristic sketches of Confederate officers and heroes, with battle-scenes and incidents in camp and field, interesting hospital experiences, suitable moral reflections, and occasional dissertations and discourses, which it is hoped will detract nothing from the merit or utility of the volume.

"These PAPERS from his PORTFOLIO are necessarily somewhat fragmentary in form, written as they were in the brief and uncertain intervals of official duty, amid frequent interruptions and manifold inconveniences, sometimes sitting upon the ground by night, with no light but the camp-fire, and no book but the Bible. In the quiet leisure of home, the work would have assumed a more consecutive character . . .

"Not aspiring to the dignity of a HISTORY OF THE WAR, this book may nevertheless serve as a quarry whence the future Historian may obtain some rough material for his work."—"Introductory," I, iii-iv.
Crandall 2620.

DABNEY, ROBERT LEWIS, 1820-1898   26

True courage: a discourse commemorative of Lieut. General Thomas J. Jackson, by Rev. R. L. Dabney, D.D., Professor in Union Theological Seminary, Va. Richmond, Va.: Presbyterian Committee of Publication of the Confederate States, 1863.
32 p. 15.5 cm.

"Appendix. Sketch of the life of Lieut. Gen. T. J. Jackson:" p. ₍27₎-32.
Crandall 2568.
There was a second edition in the same year (Crandall 2569).

The campaign from Texas to Maryland. By Rev. Nicholas A. Davis, Chaplain Fourth Texas Reg. C. S. A. Richmond: Printed at the Office of the Presbyterian Committee of Publication of the Confederate States, 1863.

165, ₁1₁ p. 2 port. (incl. front.). 19.5 cm.

Cover-title: The campaign from Texas to Maryland, with the battle of Fredericksburg.

"One of the most agreeable books published for some time. Mr. Davis sets a good example to the skilful writers in all other regiments. Every regiment, nay each company, should record its own history."—*Southern Literary Messenger,* xxxv (1863), 191.

Crandall 2621.

A second edition was issued by E. H. Cushing, Houston, Texas, 1863. 87 p. 20.5 cm. (Crandall 2622).

"We are indebted to our friend Cushing, of the Houston Telegraph, for a copy of 'The Campaign from Texas to Maryland' by Rev. N. A. Davis, Chaplain of the 4th Texas Regiment. The book contains 87 pages of closely printed matter, is well got up, and is a graphic history of the noble Texas brigade from the time it was organized, until and including the battle of Fredericksburg, on the 13th Dec. last, including biographical sketches of officers, incidents, &c. It is a book which should be in the hands of every Texan. E. H. Cushing, Publisher, Houston, Texas."— Dallas *Herald,* August 26, 1863.

₁DE BOW, JAMES DUNWOODY BROWNSON₁ 1820-1867   28

. . . The interest in slavery of the Southern non-slaveholder. The right of peaceful secession. Slavery in the Bible. Charleston: Steam-Power Presses of Evans & Cogswell, 1860.

Cover-title, 30 p. 21.5 cm.

At head of title: 1860 association. Tract, no. 5.

The first article is a letter by J. D. B. De Bow, dated Nashville, Dec. 5, 1860. The second is a letter to the Boston *Courier* of December 8, 1860, signed "Langdon." The third is "The character and influence of abolitionism, extracts from a sermon preached by Rev. Henry J. Van Dyke."

Crandall 2886.

The title page of another issue (not in Crandall or Harwell) lists the third section of the pamphlet as "The character and influence of abolitionism."

Marginalia; or, Gleanings from an army note-book. By "Personne," army correspondent of the Charles Courier. Columbia, S. C.: Steam Power-Press of F. G. DeFontaine & Co., 1864.
2 p. l., iii, 248 p. 22 cm.

"F. G. DeFontaine, one of the editors of the Columbia Carolinian, is preparing for the press a volume to be entitled 'Marginalia, or Gleanings from an Army Note Book, by "Personne," army correspondent of the Charleston Courier.' It will comprise an anecdote history of the war, embracing some six hundred pages. A limited edition will be issued, and this will be distributed exclusively among subscribers and forwarded in serials of one hundred pages each. The well known capacity of the author is a surety of the success of the promised publication."—*Southern Literary Messenger,* xxxv (1863), 191.
Crandall 2623.

FANNING, DAVID, 1756?-1825 30

The narrative of Colonel David Fanning, (a Tory in the revolutionary war with Great Britain;) giving an account of his adventures in North Carolina, from 1775 to 1783, as written by himself, with an introduction and explanatory notes. Richmond, Va.: Printed for Private Distribution Only, in the First Year of the Independnence [sic] of the Confederate States of America, 1861.
xxv, 92 p. 28.5 x 22.5 cm. (Half-title: Historical documents relating to the Old North State, no. 1 . . .)

Edited from a copy of the original manuscript by T. H. Wynne. The introduction is by John H. Wheeler. Many of the notes are by D. L. Swain.
Sixty copies printed, fifty on thin writing paper and ten on thicker paper.
W. H. Clemmitt, printer.
"True to his motto, 'Gather up the fragments that Remain,' Mr. Thos. H. Wynne, with whose name the historian and antiquarian are familiar, has printed, for private circulation, a few copies of David Fanning's Narrative of his exploits. The work is very curious and interesting, in that it gives us a rough, but exceedingly accurate photograph of the condition

of things in 'The Old North State' during the eventful period from 1775 to 1783."—*Southern Literary Messenger,* XXXIV (1862), 208.
  Crandall 2624.

FOLSOM, JAMES MADISON, 1838-   31

  Heroes and martyrs of Georgia. Georgia's record in the revolution of 1861. By James M. Folsom. Macon, Ga.: Burke, Boykin & Company, 1864.
  164 p. 22 cm.

  On cover: Volume first.
  No more published.
  "In closing up the First Volume of 'Heroes and Martyrs of Georgia,' &c., I desire to make a few explanations regarding the contents of the forthcoming volumes. I had hoped to publish . . . in *four* volumes; but . . . I have resolved to . . . add either to the size of the volumes or increase their number to six.
  "The greater portion of my MSS. having been either carried off or destroyed by the Federals in their march through Georgia, I will be compelled to revisit the army, and re-collect the material to complete my work."—"Addendum," p. ₍163₎.
  Crandall 2625.

FORD, SALLIE (ROCHESTER), 1828-1902   32

  Raids and romance of Morgan and his men, by Sally Rochester Ford . . . Mobile: S. H. Goetzel & Co., 1863.
  319 p. 20.5 cm.

  Wallpaper wrappers.
  One page of advertisements at end.
  Entered for copyright in the Court of the Southern Division of the District of Alabama April 13, 1863.
  "It gives a truthful account of the organization of Morgan's corps of partizans, and of their dashing exploits during more than a year. It is written in a fascinating style, combining with its historical accuracy the exciting interest of a first class romance."—*The Southern Field and Fireside,* n.s., I (1863), 143.
  Harwell 1025.
  A second edition was published in 1864, 332 p. (Crandall 3092).

Three months in the Southern States: April, June, 1863. By Lieut.-Col. Fremantle, Coldstream Guards. Mobile: S. H. Goetzel, 1864.

158 p. 20 cm.

Wallpaper wrappers.

"I have not attempted to conceal any of the peculiarities or defects of the Southern people. . . . I think no generous man, whatever may be his political opinions, can do otherwise than admire the courage, energy, and patriotism of the whole population, and the skill of its leaders, in this struggle against great odds."—"Preface," p. ₍3₎.

Crandall 2670.

GAMMAGE, WASHINGTON LAFAYETTE, d. 1865   34

The camp, the bivouac, and the battle field. Being a history of the Fourth Arkansas Regiment, from its first organization down to the present date: "Its campaigns and its battles." With an occasional reference to the current events of the times, including biographical sketches of its field officers and others of the "Old Brigade." The whole interspersed here and there with descriptions of scenery, incidents of camp life, etc., by W. L. Gammage, Brigade Surgeon of Mc'Nair's ₍sic₎ Brigade. Selma: Cooper & Kimball, Mississippian Book and Job Office, 1864.

164 p. 21 cm.

"Book-making has not been any part of my vocation heretofore and would not have been attempted now, but for the desire I had to perpetuate and to preserve, in some measure from oblivion, the services that my comrades, both great and simple, have rendered to the country in this war, not that I claim for what is herein written the importance which the world attaches to History in its broadest and most perfect sense, but feeling conscious that when the rigid test of scrutiny is applied to my labors, it will be found that a faithful adherence to the truth is one of its leading features. I hope I may console myself with the reflection that I have written not altogether in vain. . . .

"I have collated what is now offered to the world, from a diary which has been my constant companion and the recipient of my observations and crude thoughts from day to day, ever since the war began. . . .

"The entire work has been begun and finished in Camp, surrounded by the bustle and noise and confusion incident thereto."—"Preface."
Harwell 1038.

[GIBBES, ROBERT WILSON] 1809-1866   35
Memorial. To the Honorable the Congress of the Confederate States of America. . . . [Columbia, S. C.? 1864]
4 p. 23.5 cm.

Caption title.
Signed: R. W. Gibbes, M. D., *President Press Association C. S. A.*

"In behalf of the Press Association, comprising every daily paper issued within the limits of the Confederate States, I respectfully ask that no changes be made in the present exemption law, so far as relates to them. It is scarcely necessary to call your attention to the unquestionable fact that the vitality of our present revolution has been in the spirit of our free press —at once the expression and the conductor of the sentiment and feeling of the people, fostering, conveying, and extending their influence with a mighty power—based upon the most extraordinary unanimity that has ever characterised any people. As the chief and potent means of diffusing knowledge among the masses, and of concentrating the convictions of the public mind in relation to great principles embodying the rights and interests of man, politically, morally, and socially, the press has been engaged most successfully in proclaiming and inculcating them.

"It has ever been the pride of our Southern sovereignties that our people were educated in the great truths that are the proper basis of self-government—those principles that were adopted and established by our fathers of '76—cherished, illustrated, and enforced by means of an independent press."—p. [1].
Crandall 2749.

GILHAM, WILLIAM, 1819?-1872   36
Manual of instruction for the volunteers and militia of the Confederate States. By William Gilham, Colonel of Volunteers, Instructor of Tactics, and Commandant of Cadets, Virginia Military Institute. Richmond, Va.: West & Johnston, 1862 [c. 1861].
xxiv, [25], 559 p. 82 plates (2 fold.). 18.5 cm.

Printed by Evans & Cogswell, Charleston, S. C.
"This is one of the most invaluable and meritorious Military Publica-

tions extant. It is an accepted and standard authority with the first Military Geniuses of the Confederate States, and constitutes in itself one of the very best School Books of the Art of War in any language."—West & Johnston, *Descriptive Catalogue of Publications* ([Richmond: 1864]), p. 3.

Crandall 2419.

First edition, Richmond, 1861 (Crandall 2418). There were several abridged editions (Crandall 2415, 2416, 2417, 2420 and Harwell 947).

GOULDING, FRANCIS ROBERT, 1810-1881   37

Robert and Harold; or, The young marooners on the Florida coast. By Rev. F. R. Goulding. First Confederate; from the eighth United States edition, revised and enlarged. Macon, Ga.: Burke, Boykin & Co., Steam Book and Job Printers, 1863.
1 p. l., viii, [9]-233 p. 21 cm.

Entered for copyright in the District Court of the Southern District of Georgia May 30, 1863.

"This captivating volume, the original edition of which was read with so much avidity, North and South, as well as in Europe, where large editions were issued, has been republished by the enterprising house of Burke, Boykin & Co.

"It is a record of important truths and real incidents, thrown together in the form of a well-told tale. The whole inculcates elevating moral lessons, and may be read with pleasure and profit by all. The style in which the book is printed is highly creditable to the publishers—the printing being clearer and more uniform than any work we have seen printed during the war."—*The Southern Field and Fireside*, n. s., I (1863), 151.

"The Young Marooners is too well known for us to say more than, 'Buy it, by all means, and give it to your children to read. It will prove more interesting to them than Robinson Crusoe.'"—*The Countryman*, XIX (1864), 381.

Crandall 3129.

GREEN, DUFF, 1791-1875   38

Facts and suggestions relative to finance & currency, addressed to the President of the Confederate States. By Duff Green. Augusta, Ga.: J. T. Paterson & Co., Lithographers and Printers, 1864.
Cover-title, 80 p. incl. tables, diagrs. plate. 21.5 cm.

"I proceed first to show what money is, and will then demonstrate that Congress has power to convert the Treasury Certificates into money, by making them a legal tender. The cause for which I plead, is the cause of Civil and Religious Liberty, of right, of justice, of good faith, of pecuniary independence, of human progress and prosperity, and I beseech you, the Congress, the Legislatures of the several States, and the people, for the sake of that cause, earnestly to consider the facts and arguments which I respectfully submit in support of it."—p. 3.

Crandall 2763.

[HALLOCK, CHARLES] 1834-   39

A complete biographical sketch of "Stonewall" Jackson: giving a full and accurate account of the leading events of his military career, his dying moments, and the obsequies at Richmond and Lexington. Augusta, Ga.: Steam Power-Press Chronicle and Sentinel, 1863.

38 p., 1 l., ii p. 21 cm.

Entered for copyright in the District Court of the Southern District of Georgia June 13, 1863.

"This is the title of a well-written and concise biographical record of the leading events in the life of this idolized patriot and warrior ... It contains also many anecdotes and incidents of his life, never before given to the public. It is a most acceptable memorial of the life of this great and good man, and is admirably adapted for circulation in camp, where it will be sought after with avidity."—*The Southern Field and Fireside*, n. s., I (1863), 151.

Crandall 2578.

HARDEE, WILLIAM JOSEPH, 1815-1873   40

... Rifle and light infantry tactics, revised and improved by Col. W. J. Hardee, C. S. Army. First edition ... Mobile: S. H. Goetzel & Co., First Year of the Confederacy [1861].

2 v. fold. front., plates (part fold.). 12.5 cm.

At head of title: The only copy-right edition.

Vol. I: Schools of the soldier and company; Instruction for skirmishers. 250 p. incl. music. Vol. II: School of the battalion. 232 p.

Lithographic plates by W. R. Robertson.

One volume printed by J. Y. Thompson, the other by the Mobile Register Job Office.

Entered for copyright in the Court of the Southern Division, District of Alabama June 24, 1861.

"The lithographs are all astonishingly well done, and are pronounced by Col. Hardee to be better than those in the Philadelphia edition of the Lippincotts. . . .

"[T]his is the only edition which is authorized by the author himself . . . and it is the first copyright under the Confederate States of America. This edition is the only one which contains all the improvements and changes which the author recently made.

"In the face of all these advantages, several spurious editions . . . have been put upon the public. . . . If publishers do not respect rights like these, we ask, what will hereafter be the value of a copyright in the Confederate States of America?"—Mobile *Register & Advertiser*, June 27, 1861.

Crandall 2422.

Volume I of another edition was printed for Goetzel by Thompson, with exactly the same wording on the title page but measuring 21.5 cm., prior to the publication of this edition (Crandall 2421). It was entered for copyright in the Court of the Southern Division, District of Alabama May 4, 1861. Goetzel published five editions by the end of 1861 and nine by the end of 1863 (Crandall 2421-2429). Other Confederate editions were published by the Southern Publishing House of Hutton & Freligh (Memphis: 1861); E. C. Kirk & Co. (Memphis: 1861); J. O. Griffith & Co., Union and American Office (Nashville, Tenn.: 1861); H. P. Lathrop (New-Orleans: 1861); J. W. Randolph (Richmond, Va.: 1861); Texas Printing House, E. W. Cave (Houston: 1863); J. Spelman, Printer to the State (Raleigh, N. C.: 1862); Power and Cadwallader Book and Job Printers (Jackson, Miss.: 1861); True Democrat Steam Press Print. (Little Rock: 1862). (Crandall 2430-2439; Harwell 948, 949).

[HAW, MARY JANE]   41

The rivals, a Chickahominy story. By Miss M. J. H., of Virginia. Illustrated. Richmond: Ayres & Wade, 1864.
61 p. incl. plates. 21.5 cm.

Winner of $1,000 as the "Prize Story" of *The Southern Illustrated News*. Published serially in the *Illustrated News* beginning April 23, 1864 (III, no. 16).
Crandall 3093.

War: a poem with copious notes. Founded on the revolution of 1861-62 (up to the battles before Richmond inclusive). By John H. Hewitt . . . Richmond: West & Johnston, 1862.

vi, [7]-85 p. 23 cm.

R. W. Gibbes, printer, Columbia, S. C.

"As a whole—though professing to be only a hurried production, it is a valuable contribution to the war literature of the day."—*The Southern Field and Fireside*, n. s., I (1863), 92.

Crandall 3140.

Les misérables. (The wretched.) A novel. By Victor Hugo. A new translation, revised. In five parts: I. Fantine. II. Cosette. III. Marius. IV. St. Denis. V. Jean Valjean . . . Richmond: West & Johnston, 1863-64.

5 v. 22.5 cm.

Part title at head of cover-title.

"Price two dollars" noted on covers, pts. 1-4.

"'Les Miserables,' says the *Literary Messenger*, 'is to us a Bible in fictitious literature of the nineteenth century; it is a protest of Genius against universal crimes—the plea of one who advocates in the face of obloquy and contumely, the cause of the life-wretched. It is a good sermon in behalf of primitive Christianity—beautiful as the *Iliad* of Homer, real as a play by Shakespeare. Les Miserables is an event—it is a new jewel in the literary coronet of our century."—West & Johnston, *Descriptive Catalogue of Publications* ([Richmond: 1864]), p. 13.

Crandall 3096.

The life and times of Bertrand DuGuesclin: a history of the fourteenth century. By D. F. Jamison of South Carolina. Charleston: John Russell, 1864.

2 v. 22 cm.

"We have said that the style of this history is somewhat dry, and that its materials, though well arranged, are not digested—that the author has rather reproduced and modernised the history given us by the old chroniclers than written one of his own by the aid of their information. But this said, we have said all that can be said in dispraise of a work whose merits we by no means desire to underrate. If it be not exactly light reading, it is not made otherwise by any affectation of style or substance; it is perfectly free from pretension of every kind, and the story of a great man, better appreciated in his own time than by posterity, is told as his contemporaries told it, with few comments and no embellishment. This is all Mr. Jamison pretends to do; he has done it under considerable disadvantages, and he has done it well, and his work is likely to restore to its deserved place in the temple of fame a name which has been deprived of honours freely bestowed on much less deserving claimants."—*The Index* (London), IV (1864), 474-75.

Crandall 2587.

[JOHNSTON, RICHARD MALCOLM] 1822-1898   45

Georgia sketches; containing Mr. Israel Meadows and his school, Judge Mike and his court, How Bill Williams took the responsibility, Miss Pea, Miss Spouter and the Yankee. From the recollections of an old man. By Philemon Perch . . . [Augusta, Ga.:] Published by Stockton & Co., 1864.
114 p. 20 cm.

Dedication in title.
"This is the title of a Georgia book, by a Georgia author, issued by a Georgia Publishing House. We acknowledge the receipt of a copy of the work, from our friend the author, with peculiar pleasure, and promise ourself a treat from its perusal, part of which we have already enjoyed as it was served up in the columns of a Georgia journal [*The Southern Field and Fireside*]. The author of the work is a gentleman of finished belles lettres attainments."—*The Countryman*, XIX (1864), 520.

JONES, CHARLES COLCOCK, 1804-1863   46

Religious instruction of the Negroes. An address delivered before the General Assembly of the Presbyterian Church, at Augusta, Ga., December 10, 1861. By Rev. C. C. Jones, D.D. Published by order of the General Assembly. Richmond: Presbyterian Committee of Publication [1862].
25 p. 15 cm.

Caption title.

"The importance of the instruction of the negroes under our present circumstances cannot be too highly estimated. Is it too much to say that the stability and welfare of both Church and State depend largely upon it? My brethren, the eyes of the civilized world are upon us. There are but two other nations beside our own that hold in their bosoms the institution of slavery. Ponder that fact and the responsibilities involved in it. None can come in from abroad to relieve us. The negroes of the Confederate States are thrown entirely upon the care of the churches of our Lord within those States. The Christian world outside looks to us to do our duty, and, more than that, *God our Saviour looks to us to do our duty.* You feel the weighty responsibility; you say by the help of God we must meet it, and meet it in the very *birthday* of our existence as the Presbyterian Church in the Confederate States of America. Then let the Presbyterian Church in the Confederate States awake and pray for the baptism of the Holy Spirit, and put on her strength; ministers, elders and members, awake, gird up your loins and quit yourselves like men. Our brethren of other denominations will awake and act also; so that we shall emulate each other's zeal, and there shall be action and re-action in all the Zion of God, and higher and higher shall rise our zeal in so good a cause, and greater and greater become our labors, until our whole population shall be evangelized, and our whole land be filled with the glory of the Lord."—p. 24-25.

Crandall 2888.

JONES, JOHN BEAUCHAMP, 1810-1866   47

Wild western scenes; or, The white spirit of the wilderness. Being a narrative of adventures, embracing the same characters portrayed in the original "Wild western scenes," over one hundred editions of which have been sold in Europe and America. By J. B. Jones, author of the first series of "Wild western scenes." New series. Richmond: M. A. Malsby, 1863.

iv, 123, [1] p. 19 cm.

Macfarlane & Fergusson, printers.

"NOTE:—Owing to the destruction, by fire of the Bath Paper Mills near Hamburg, S. C., the Publisher has been disappointed in getting such a quantity of book paper as would justify in publishing the entire work at this time, and therefore, has been compelled to issue it in two volumes, the second of which is now in press and will be out as soon as the necessary supply of paper can be procured.

"Hoping the above explanation will be satisfactory, the Publisher asks the indulgence of a generous public while he endeavors to overcome the difficulties of home enterprizes."—verso p. 123.

"It is full of humor and a dashing spirit of adventure."—*The Southern Field and Fireside*, n. s., I (1863), 142.

Crandall 3098.

JOYNES, EDWARD SOUTHEY, 1834-1917   48

Education after the war: a letter addressed to a member of the Southern Educational Convention, Columbia, S. C., 28th April, 1863. By Edward S. Joynes, A. M., Professor of Greek Literature in William and Mary College, Va. Published in the Southern Literary Messenger, and re-printed for the use of the Convention. Richmond: Macfarlane & Fergusson, Printers, 1863.
16 p. 20 cm.

First published in the *Southern Literary Messenger*, XXXV (1863), 485-492.

"Such a revolution cannot pass in the history of any people, without deeply affecting the character, not only of the living, but of future generations, and manifesting its influence for ages to come, in all the relations of social and domestic, as well as political, life. What the nature of this influence will be, in its moral aspects, it is important to inquire in advance; an inquiry, which in the midst of the overwhelming interests and passions of the existing crisis, would be unheeded by the general public, but which it behooves those, who, being the professed Educators of the people, are the appointed Cultivators and Guardians of those moral influences, which form and impress the character of the young, carefully to consider; and which, unless *they anticipate*, will be but too late regarded by other men. The proposed Convention, in which teachers from all parts of the country will be assembled in conference, seems to me to afford an opportune occasion for the consideration of this question, and for the interchange of such views, and the discussion and determination of such principles of education, as shall prepare teachers to meet in their sphere, not the least important, the momentous duties of the present and coming age. To this end, I respectfully propose to offer, for your consideration, a few thoughts, which your own experience may, I trust, make practically useful."—p. 6-7.

"Education after the War

Is the title of a letter addressed to a member of the Southern Educational Convention at Columbia, S. C., by Professor Edward S. Joynes. This is an exceedingly able paper, upon one of the most vital interests of the country. Professor Joynes is well known in Virginia as one of the most accomplished of our professional literary men. As Professor of Greek literature in the venerable college of William & Mary before the war, and in other positions of public usefulness, he has given evidence of abilities and attainments of a high character. He rightly says that those matters which pertain to our educational interests are 'next in importance to the war itself, in which we are staked our existence and our liberties.'"—*Southern Literary Messenger*, XXXVI (1864), 318.

Crandall 3996.

KEATINGE & BALL, *bank note engravers*, Columbia, South Carolina 49

Remarks on the manufacture of bank notes, and other promises to pay. Addressed to the bankers of the Southern Confederacy. Columbia, S. C.: Steam Power-Press of F. G. DeFontaine & Co., 1864.

31 p. front. 23 cm.

Frontispiece is a montage of devices used by Keatinge & Ball on the Confederate bonds and other notes manufactured by that firm.

"It is in the want of material that the prosecution of bank note engraving and printing in the Confederacy has met with the greatest difficulties. Many of the most important articles are not to be obtained in Europe of the quality desired; others have to be devised, as it were, on the spot. The swamps of South Carolina furnish the vegetable carbon for the inks, and the hills of North Carolina and Virginia, the oils. Plates and dies ₍are₎ made from the crude steel. The manufacture of machinery and presses gives employment to mechanism of an entirely novel character in the South; in fact, to establishments of this kind, necessity has added to the machine shop the laboratory of the chemist.

"... The progress made, under these difficulties and peculiarities, in the Confederacy is, therefore, gratifying, and gives assurance that when the clouds of war are dissipated, the commerce of the whole world admitted again to our silent wharves, and peace, with healing wings, brings health, activity, and her innumerable blessings to the once happy people of the Confederacy, this important branch of industry will take its legitimate rank, bestowing its benefits upon the commonwealth, as well as honor and profit upon those engaged in its prosecution."—p. 31-32.

Crandall 2919.

Prisoner of war; or, Five months among the Yankees. Being a narrative of the crosses, calamities, and consolations of a Petersburg militiaman during an enforced summer residence north. By A. Rifleman, esq., gent. Richmond, Va.: West & Johnston [1865]. 120 p. 22.5 cm.

"This is also a narrative of Prison adventures, and as a companion to Mr. Pollard's work [item 68 in this list], is invaluable in arriving at accurate conclusions respecting the opinions, hopes, prospects and designs of the Northern people in their war for subjugation. A perusal of the two publications (this work and Mr. Pollard's) will give the advantage to be derived from opinions formed at different standpoints of observation, and will furnish all the information necessary to intelligent conclusions as to the various subjects pertaining to the war. This publication of Messrs. West & Johnston is unsurpassed in its literary character by any work that we have read for years. It has all the thrilling interest of a legend of romance, and its beauties of composition are eminently worthy of the accomplished gentleman to whom its authorship is accredited."— *The Evening Courier*, Richmond, March 24, 1865.

Crandall 2637.

LAMAR, LUCIUS QUINTUS CINCINNATUS, 1825-1893   51

Speech of Hon. L. Q. C. Lamar, of Miss., on the state of the country. Delivered in the Atheneum, Atlanta, Ga., Thursday evening, April 14, 1864. Reported by A. E. Marshall. Published by request. Atlanta, Ga.: J. J. Toon & Co., Publishers, Franklin Steam Printing House, 1864.
30 p. 20 cm.

Crandall 2780.

LECONTE, JOHN, 1818-1891   52

How to make salt from sea-water. By Professor John LeConte. Published by the Governor and Council of South Carolina. Columbia, S. C.: Charles P. Pelham, State Printer, 1862.
10 p. 21 cm.

Crandall 2923.

LIFE OF JAMES W. JACKSON, the Alexandria hero, the slayer of Ells-
worth, the first martyr in the cause of Southern independence;
containing a full account of the circumstances of his heroic death,
and the many remarkable incidents of his eventful life, constituting a true history, more like romance than reality. Published for
the benefit of his family. Richmond: West & Johnston, 1862. 53
48 p. 21.5 cm.

Macfarlane & Fergusson, printers.
"If any explanation be necessary by the author of a work so eminently
proper as this, of the hopes which have induced its publication, it is all
happily contained in the following letter:

'VIRGINIA SENATE CHAMBER, *Feby* 5th, 1862

'Capt. ————.
'Dear Sir:
'I have examined with care the manuscript of the life of my late
brother-in-law, James W. Jackson, which you have submitted to me. I
find that you have portrayed graphically and truthfully the many stirring
incidents in his truly wonderful career.

'Satisfied that the many acts of daring and self-sacrificing devotion to
our holy cause which adorned the closing scenes of my brother's life will
be, to our Southern youth, an inspiration to fire their zeal; trusting that
the desire to know them, among our people, may prove of benefit to his
stricken family; and convinced of its necessity as a matter of public history, I heartily approve of the publication of your work, and wish you
every success.

Yours very truly,
HENRY W. THOMAS,
Representative 24th Senatorial District.'" —

"Prefatory." p. ₍3₎.
Crandall 2590.

McCABE, JAMES DABNEY, 1842-1883   54
The aid-de-camp: a romance of the war. By James D. McCabe,
Jr. Richmond: W. A. J. Smith, 1863.
113 p. 23 cm.

Macfarlane & Fergusson, printers.
Originally published in *The Magnolia Weekly*, Richmond.

"The romance of 'THE AID-DE-CAMP,'" was written during the fall of 1862, more for the purpose of beguiling a season of weariness than with the expectation of presenting it to the public. It was originally published in 'The Magnolia Weekly,' and the great success with which it met there has encouraged the Author to attempt a re-publication, this time in its present form.

"It is now offered to the public with the hope that it may meet with new friends and additional success.

"RICHMOND, VA., 10th of August, 1863."

"We are constantly receiving orders for back numbers of our paper containing this romance.—The demand for the story has become so great, Messrs. Smith & Barrow have purchased the copyright from the author and the book is now in press."—*The Magnolia Weekly*, I (1863), 280.

"The above is highly spoken of—is very cheap for the times [$2.00], and has, we hear, sold largely."—*Southern Literary Messenger*, xxxv (1863), 748.

Crandall 3104.

McCABE, JAMES DABNEY, 1842-1883   55

. . . The guerillas: an original domestic drama, in three acts. By James D. McCabe, Jr. With cast of characters, stage business, costumes, relative positions, &c., by R. D'Orsey Ogden, acting and stage manager of Richmond Varieties and New Richmond Theatre. Richmond: West & Johnston, 1863.
Cover-title, 44 p. 19 cm.

At head of title: West & Johnston's standard drama.

"First original drama produced in the Confederacy; played for the first time at the Richmond Varieties, on Monday evening, Dec. 22nd, 1862. Was 'enthusiastically received by the public, and had a successful run for an entire week.'"—*Southern Literary Messenger*, xxxv (1863), 192.

Crandall 3228.

[McDONALD, WILLIAM NAYLOR] 1834-1898   56

The two rebellions; or, Treason unmasked. By a Virginian. Richmond: Smith, Bailey & Co., 1865.
144 p. 19.5 cm.

"The outbreak at the Ferry was the first rebellion, with John Brown for its nominal leader. The second, though plotted for a long time, was publicly organized by Seward, Greeley & co., at Chicago, the following year."—p. 112.

Crandall 2638.

MCHENRY, GEORGE   57

... A paper containing a statement of facts relating to the approaching cotton crisis. By George McHenry. Richmond, Dec. 31, 1864. ₁Richmond: 1865₁.

87 p. 22.5 cm.

At head of title: House of representatives. Secret session.
Caption title: The cotton crisis.
Letter on p. ₁3₁ dated: Richmond, January 8, 1865.
Crandall 2927.

MACMAHON, T. W.   58

Cause and contrast: an essay on the American crisis. By T. W. MacMahon. Richmond, Va.: West & Johnston, 1862 ₁c.1861₁.

xv, 192 p. 22 cm.

C. H. Wynne, printer.
"'The author treats all subjects growing out of the slavery dispute with an acuteness of analysis and a grace of style that give a wonderful freshness to subjects which have become hackneyed by other writers, and has produced in the whole a popular and graceful exposition of Southern political philosophy.'—*Richmond Examiner*."—Publishers' advertisement, inside back wrapper of the *Southern Literary Messenger*, XXXIV (1862), no. 1.

Crandall 2784.

MAHAN, DENNIS HART   59

Summary of the course of permanent fortification and of the attack and defence of permanent works, for the use of the cadets of the U. S. Military Academy. By D. H. Mahan, Professor of Military Engineering, etc., etc. Richmond: West & Johnston, 1863.

352 p. 23 cm.

Evans & Cogswell, printers, No. 3 Broad street, Charleston, S. C.

"The publishers do not exaggerate, when they say that this is the most splendid, elaborate, scientific, and indispensable book ever printed in the South. It is an exact reprint from the West Point lithographic Edition, which was exclusively printed for the use of that institution, containing 32 beautifully lithographed plates; size; 20 inches, 17 inches.

"The printing was done by Evans & Cogswell of Charleston, whose bookwork rivals that of the famous Riverside press at Cambridge; the paper is excellent and the binding neat and tasty. For a people engaged as we are in defensive warfare against a powerful foe, this magnificent work may be regarded as a national benefaction."—*Southern Literary Messenger*, xxxv (1863), 127.

Crandall 2458.

West & Johnston had published in 1862 the volume of plates designed to accompany this volume: *Plates to Summary of the course of permanent fortifications and of the attack and defence of permanent works....* The plates are in two series of nine and twenty-three. The first series is framed at 19 x 22.5 cm. on sheets 24.5 cm. The second series measures 34.5 cm. The second series is signed: B. Duncan, litho, Columbia, S. C. (Crandall 2455).

Two other editions with the same paging were published by Evans & Cogswell, 1862 and 1863 (Crandall 2456 and 2457).

MARMONT, AUGUSTE FRÉDÉRIC LOUIS VIESSE DE, *duc de Raguse,* 1774-1852   60

The spirit of military institutions. By Marshal Marmont, Duc de Ragusa. Translated from the last Paris edition (1859), and augmented by biographical, historical, topographical, and military notes; with a new version of General Jomini's celebrated thirty-fifth chapter, of part I, of Treatise on grand military operations, by Frank Schaller, Colonel 22d Mississippi, Confederate Army. Columbia, S. C.: Evans & Cogswell, 1864.
278 p. 17.5 cm.

"To you, Mr. President, whose genius has not *only* organized an army but has achieved the still greater task of *maintaining* and *strengthening* it, amid circumstances the most unfavorable, until it has become in numbers, spirit, devotion, and efficiency, more formidable than it has ever before been, even after a period of over thirty months of active warfare—to you, then, whose achievements in this respect alone make you a master of the art of war, I have proposed, and herewith most respectfully beg permission, to dedicate my work."—p. 10.

Crandall 2462.

MARSHALL, ALEXANDER J. 61

Five chapters of an unpublished "Book for the times;" giving a Virginia view of the causes of the revolution in the border slave states. And demonstrating who were the true authors of the Civil War. By A. J. Marshall. Richmond: James E. Goode, Printer, 1863.

40 p. 23 cm.

"The chapters of my book, which I propose now to publish, fully sustain the course of the border slave states on these high grounds of moral right and of eminent state necessity. But the argument to establish this position also involves a critical analysis of the acts and motives of President Lincoln and of the republican leaders. To sift the gloss with which he sanded the eyes of the North, whilst he inflamed their passions, from his real but covert design of war upon slavery, is my second purpose in publishing these chapters at the present time."—p. 4.

"I have thought that a Virginia view of this war and of its causes, which traces its responsibility by arguments absolutely demonstrative, to the Lincoln administration, might gain circulation at the North, and might aid to promote this returning justice and good sense. It is the hope of doing good by this vindication of the border slave states, and by the exposure of the artful schemes and devices by which the republicans succeeded to involve the country in a war for emancipation, that I now publish these chapters."—p. 5.

Crandall 2639.

MICHELBACHER, MAXIMILIAN J., 1811?-1879 62

A sermon delivered on the day of prayer, recommended by the President of the C. S. of A., the 27th of March, 1863, at the German Hebrew Synagogue, "Bayth Ahabah," by the Rev. M. J. Michelbacher. Richmond: Macfarlane & Fergusson, 1863.

16 p. 23 cm.

Crandall 4169.

Catalogue of imported goods to be sold at auction, by Wilkes Morris, auctioneer. Commencing on Thursday, Dec. 17th, 1863, at 9 o'clock. A.M., at No. 2 Granite Row,—Front Street, Wilmington, N. C. Conditions—Cash on delivery. Wilmington, N. C.: Printed on the Journal Steam Power Press, 1863.
Cover-title, 20 p. 31.5 cm.

On back wrapper: "Rules and conditions of sale."
Harwell 1139.

NOEL, THEOPHILUS 64

A campaign from Santa Fe to the Mississippi; being a history of the old Sibley Brigade from its first organization to the present time; its campaigns in New Mexico, Arizona, Texas, Louisiana and Arkansas, in the years 1861-2-3-4. By Theo Noel, 4th Texas Cavalry. Shreveport, La.: Shreveport News Printing Establishment—John Dickinson, proprietor, 1865.
152 p. fold. table. 19 cm.

"This work, kind reader, which is now presented to you, was born in the tented field, amid the din and confusion of a soldiers camp. By piece-meals—a paragraph here, a sentence or more somewhere else—after stopping in the very centre of one to perform the duties incumbent upon me as a private soldier in the ranks, has my work been moulded. Having no other aim in view than that of truthfulness, this work is presented to you, not for your criticism, but, if possible, to lay before the reading world and our friends in the 'Lone Star State' an account of what we, as your sons, have done since we espoused for the achievement of our common liberties."—"Apology, Preface and Introduction,"—p. ₍3₎.

"Kind Reader, the work has commenced; I have undertaken to compile for your especial benefit a history of our Brigade and its doings. The world has been furnished with 'The Campaign from Texas to Maryland,' by the Rev. Mr. Davis, of the Fourth Texas Infantry, and 'The Camp, the Bivouac, and the Battle-field,' by Dr. Gammage, of the Fourth Arkansas; 'The first, second, third, and perhaps the fourth years of the war,' by Pollard; and why not now with that of the Old Sibley—Green—Hardeman Brigade. May I hope that this—my first offering—may in part be favored and appreciated by the friends of that Old Brigade throughout the 'Lone Star State.'"—p. ₍5₎.
Crandall 2642.

A sermon: preached before Brig.-Gen. Hoke's brigade, at Kinston, N. C., on the 28th of February, 1864, by Rev. John Paris, upon the death of twenty-two men, who had been executed in the presence of the brigade for the crime of desertion. Greensborough, N. C.: A. W. Ingold & Co., Book and Job Printers, 1864. 1 p. l., [5]-15 p. 15.5 cm.

"After their execution I thought it proper, for the benefit of the living, that I should deliver a discourse before our brigade, upon the death of these men, that the eyes of the living might be opened, to view the horrid and ruinous crime and sin of desertion, which had become so prevalent. A gentleman from Forsyth county, who was present at the delivery of the discourse, solicited a copy for publication, which has been granted."— p. [4].

Crandall 4177.

Elements of seamanship. Prepared as a text book for the midshipmen of the C. S. Navy. By Wm. H. Parker, commanding C. S. School-ship Patrick Henry. Richmond: Macfarlane and Fergusson, 1864. xi, 189 p. 17.5 cm.

"The following work on practical Seamanship has been *compiled* from various authorities, arranged as a Text Book, and as much original matter introduced as the subject admitted of.

"It was undertaken with great reluctance, owing to the loss of all previous notes on the subject, and a press of official duties; the impossibility of procuring a Text Book for the Midshipmen under my command, however, induced me to attempt it.

"It is intended to *precede* the work on HARBOR ROUTINE and may be regarded as the development of PART I. of that book.

"Several subjects, as *Clearing Hawse, Mooring, Shifting Spars and Sails*, &c., &c., are not treated of because they had already been fully described in my MS. Seamanship on *Evolutions*, used at the U. S. Naval Academy; should I succeed in recovering a copy of that work, it is my intention to publish it as PART III. of the subject. The three books will, I believe, be found a tolerably complete treatise on Seamanship and an officer's duties.

"Not having been able to read the proof sheets of this, I fear that many typographical errors will occur; they will, however, be corrected in the next edition.

"C. S. SCHOOL-SHIP PATRICK HENRY.
James River, May, 1864."—p. ₍iii₎.
Crandall 2466.

POLLARD, EDWARD ALFRED, 1831-1872   67

The first year of the war. By Edward A. Pollard . . . Richmond: West & Johnston, 1862.
viii, ₍17₎-374 p. 23 cm.

Chas. H. Wynne, printer.
"The following tribute to this Book is from the gifted pen of the authoress of 'Beulah' ₍Augusta Jane (Evans) Wilson₎:
"'If any evidence, not palpable to the most obtuse, were required of the fixed and solemn resolution of the people of the Confederacy, and the cool, calm deliberation pervading the public mind in the midst of the gigantic revolution now being consummated, it might be furnished by the welcome appearance at this crisis, of Mr. Pollard's valuable book— a succinct, eloquent, impartial history of events, laboriously compiled in close proximity to the theatre of war, while the author looked down on the great Richmond echiquier. The work bears none of the marks of hasty structure, which might, under the exciting circumstances of its composition, be readily pardoned; on the contrary, it is characterized by remarkable unity, and by an easy, graceful diction, perspicuity and happy continuity of narration. The public will doubtless applaud and appreciate the absence in this work of the procrustean standard of favoritism, by which too many historians lop off or stretch the facts discussed, and will value the stern impartiality which manifests itself in the utterance of unpleasant but indisputable truths. The fearless meteing out of censure, just where abundant testimony fixes it, cannot fail to excite the admiration of every true, manly, honest soul. The extremes of indiscriminate praise or abuse have been avoided; but that noble moral courage, so lamentably rare in the Confederacy, which dares to lay the lash of just censure on the shoulder of the highest officials when sanctioned by irrefragable proof, seems to be possessed in an extraordinary degree by the author of this compilation of national events.'"—West & Johnston, *Descriptive Catalogue of Publications* (₍Richmond: 1864₎), p. 14.

Cover-title, item 39.

Title page, item 34.

A SERMON:

PREACHED BEFORE

Brig.-Gen. Hoke's Brigade,

AT KINSTON, N. C., ON THE 28th OF FEBRUARY, 1864,

BY Rev. JOHN PARIS,

CHAPLAIN FIFTY-FOURTH REGIMENT N. C. TROOPS,

UPON THE DEATH OF TWENTY-TWO MEN,

WHO HAD BEEN EXECUTED IN THE PRESENCE OF THE BRIGADE
FOR THE CRIME OF DESERTION.

GREENSBOROUGH, N. C.

A. W. INGOLD & CO., BOOK AND JOB PRINTERS.
1864.

WEST & JOHNSTON'S STANDARD DRAMA.

THE GUERRILLAS:

An Original Domestic Drama,

IN THREE ACTS.

By JAMES D. McCABE, Jr.

WITH CAST OF CHARACTERS, STAGE BUSINESS, COSTUMES, RELATIVE
POSITIONS, &c., BY R. D'ORSEY OGDEN, ACTING AND STAGE
MANAGER OF RICHMOND VARIETIES AND
NEW RICHMOND THEATRE.

RICHMOND:
WEST & JOHNSTON, 145 MAIN STREET.
1863.

"This ₍the third edition₎ is a corrected and improved edition of a work which we noticed at length when it first appeared. The verdict passed upon it by the public is a call for a third edition of 5000 copies—a most extraordinary sale of a book in the 'unlettered and barbarous' South. We have had time only to read Mr. Pollard's preface. He says it was written 'without heat.' Gramercy! What would become of 'Jefferson Davis,' (as Mr. P. Calls him,) and his sycophants, if Mr. Pollard should happen to rise above his ordinary temperature? They would melt away like wax in a flame.

"Contemporary history may always be erroneous, because it is necessarily partially incomplete; and opinion may differ as to Mr. Pollard's criticism, but all must agree that he is no flatterer, and that his book is singularly vivacious and attractive."—*Southern Literary Messenger*, XXXIV (1862), 591.

Crandall 2643.

"Corrected & improved edition," 1862: 2 p. l., 389 p. port., map. (Crandall 2644). "Corrected and improved edition," 1862: xvi, 17-406 p. (Crandall 2645). "Third edition," 1863: 2 p. l., viii, 406 p. (Crandall 2646).

Continued as *The Second Year of the War* (Richmond: West & Johnston, 1863): x, 17-326 p. (Crandall 2650, 2651). The succeeding *The Third Year of the War* was not published in the Confederacy but was first issued by Saunders, Otley & Co., London, 1865, and republished in the same year by C. B. Richardson, New York, who had also published editions of the first two volumes. The series was completed in 1866 by Richardson's publication of *The Last Year of the War*. Pollard's overall history of the war, *The Lost Cause*, was also published in 1866, by E. B. Treat & Co., New York.

POLLARD, EDWARD ALFRED, 1831-1872   68

Observations in the North: eight months in prison and on parole. By Edward A. Pollard. Richmond: E. W. Ayres, 1865.
vii, ₍9₎-142 p. 20.5 cm.

"We have read this last work of Mr. Pollard with the interest and instruction which are to be found in all his publications, and have risen from its perusal with more enlarged and matured views respecting the war than in our opinion could possibly be derived from the opinions of ordinary travellers and sojourners among the enemy. The public is so well acquainted with the striking features of Mr. Pollard's style of composition, that it is quite unnecessary to commend this last work from his pen as unusually readable, maintaining throughout an uninterrupted and unflagging interest. Anecdote, grave discussion of military and civil policy and prospects are gracefully blended with the well known literary attractions which belong to all the productions of Mr. Pollard's pen.

"We cannot but believe that this work, if extensively circulated and read, will exact a vast influence, of a favorable character, upon the spirits and hopes of the Southern armies and people. The press of the Confederacy cannot better serve the cause than by promoting its circulation. Mr. Pollard enjoyed abundant opportunity to acquaint himself with the spirit and resources of the North, and his opinions may be accepted with the confidence which is due to the impressions of an accurate and astute observer. Our soldiers and people will find in them abundant reason for brave resolution and unwavering hope in the eventual security of Confederate liberties, at the same time that we are compelled to accept his assurance of the necessity of continued resistance, so long as we can boast one remaining vestige of manhood."—*The Evening Courier*, Richmond, March 24, 1865.

Crandall 2647.

A second printing was completed, but not in time to be distributed to Confederate readers. It can be identified by p. 136, on which the numeral 6 in the page number has dropped below its proper place. Attached to the front wrapper is the following printed notice:

"A Relic of the Rebellion;

"The last book published in the Confederacy. . . . ₍Title, etc.₎

"This work is valuable to the antiquarian as well as to the general reader. It is the last book published in the South while under rebel rule, and is gotten up in the primitive style peculiar to Southern publications since the breaking out of the rebellion. Besides possessing value as a relic, it is an interesting narrative of the writer's capture while on his way to England on board the blockade-runner 'Greyhound,' his subsequent confinement in Fort Warren, and his treatment at the hands of the semi-secesh people of Boston and other Northern cities while on parole. The pamphlet was written and published by Mr. Pollard after his release by our authorities. A small edition was sold in the South, and a second issued; but the occupation of that city by our armies prevented its further sale. The whole edition (several hundred) was bought up by the subscriber, who entered the rebel capital in company with our victorious troops.

"A. R. Henry,
"*Correspondent New York Tribune.*"

Resources of the Southern fields and forests, medical, economical, and agricultural. Being also a medical botany of the Confederate States; with practical information on the useful properties of the trees, plants, and shrubs. By Francis Peyre Porcher, Surgeon, P. A. C. S. Prepared and published by order of the Surgeon-General, Richmond, Va. Charleston: Steam-Power Press of Evans & Cogswell, 1863.
xxv, 601 p. 22.5 cm.

"This is, in reality, one of the most splendidly useful Books ever printed in America. What Audubon did for our Ornithology, that Dr. Porcher has done for our Vegetable Kingdom. His is, indeed, a great Work; and no chemist, farmer, doctor or educated gentleman, who would know the graces of God to this favored Confederacy, can well dispense with it."—West & Johnston, *Descriptive Catalogue of Publications* ([Richmond: 1864]), p. 18.

"We incline to the opinion that a more useful work has never been issued from the American press. It is especially valuable at this time of apparent stint in the economical resources of the Confederate States . . . Here is matter for encouragement in the resolute continuance of resistance to tyranny and hostile invasion, matter for daily gratitude and praise."—*The Southern Illustrated News*, i, no. 33 (April 18, 1863), p. 2.
Crandall 3041.
Another edition: Richmond: West & Johnston, 1863 (Crandall 3042).

Press Association of the Confederate States of America 70
. . . The press association of the Confederate States of America. 1. Introduction. 2. Organization of press association. 3. Constitution. 4. Minutes of board of directors—1st session. 5. Rules of press association. 6. Minutes of board of directors—2d session. 7. Report of superintendent. 8. General instructions and rules for press reports. Printed by order of the board of directors. Griffin, Georgia: Hill & Swayze's Printing House, 1863.
56 p. 22 cm.

At head of title: Private.
"The imperfect arrangements for news reports by telegraph had long

been a subject of consideration by the Press, and at an early period of the present war, the idea became generally prevalent, that the Press should, through its own organization, choose its agents, place them where they were needed, fix their salaries, and make its own contracts with the telegraph companies."—p. ₅⟨5⟩₎.

Crandall 3284.

PRESTON, MARGARET (JUNKIN), 1820-1897   71

Beechenbrook, a rhyme of the war. By Mrs. Margaret J. Preston. Richmond: J. W. Randolph, 1865.
64 p. 18.5 cm.

Macfarlane & Fergusson, printers.

> "What need for dismay? Let the live surges roar,
> And leap in their fury, our fastnesses o'er,
> And threaten our beautiful Valley to sweep
> With the besom of ruin, most dire, and deep;—
> What fear we?—See Jackson! his sword in his hand,
> Like the stern rocks around him, immovable stand,—
> The wisdom, the skill and the strength that he boasts,
> Sought ever from him who is Leader of Hosts."—p. 35.

Crandall 3149.

QUINTARD, CHARLES TODD, 1824-1896   72

Balm for the weary and the wounded. By Rev. C. T. Quintard, chaplain 1st Tenn. Reg't, C. S. A. Columbia: Evans & Cogswell, Printers, 1864.
Cover-title, 85 p. 14 cm.

"In the left pocket of ⌜General Polk's⌝ coat was found his Book of Common-Prayer, and the right four copies of a little manual entitled 'Balm for the Weary and Wounded.' Upon the fly-leaf of three of these had been written the names respectively of 'General Jos. E. Johnston,' 'Lieutenant-General Hardee,' 'Lieutenant-General Hood,' 'with the compliments of Lieutenant-General Leonidas Polk, June 12th, 1864.' Upon that of the fourth was inscribed his own name. All were saturated with his blood."—Augusta, Georgia. Saint Paul's Church. *Funeral Services at the Burial of the Right Rev. Leonidas Polk* ... (Columbia, S. C.: 1864), p. 6.

Crandall 4234.

Notes on making saltpetre from the earth of the caves. By Major Geo. W. Rains, Corps of Artillery and Ordnance, in charge of the Gunpowder Department, C. S. A., late of the U. S. A. and former Ast. Prof. Chemistry, &c. U. S. M. A. Augusta, Ga.: Steam Power Press Chronicle & Sentinel, 1861.
12 p. 22 cm.

"The process of making Saltpetre from the earth of the limestone caves in the Southern Confederacy is so simple that anyone residing in the neighborhood of a cave in a limestone rock—and nearly all the caves are in such rock—can without any expense make at least a few pounds of the salt every day, and with assistance could make it a very profitable business at the price which the Government is now paying. To furnish the practical information required, in plain language, to such persons, so as to enable each one to add to the production of an article so indispensable to the military operations of our country, now struggling for its free existence, induces the writer to publish these notes; he would earnestly appeal to his countrymen who may live near any cave, to put themselves, if need be, to some inconvenience, in order to aid in the invaluable production. We cannot be too thankful that this gigantic war was entered upon with large supplies of ammunition and the materials for its fabrication, but little of which has yet been expended; but in a contest of such magnitude, where we have to supply the fiery food for some two thousand mouths of large dimensions—some of which consume not less than three-fourths of a keg of powder at each charge—it will readily be seen that the most abundant source of stores must fail sooner or later, unless care be taken in time to replenish the demands of consumption.

"Our supplies of sulphur—and, of course, charcoal—are probably ample for the entire war, even if it be of long duration, and the amount of saltpetre in the earth of the Southern caves, to be had for the washing is abundantly sufficient to meet all demands for an indefinite period of time."—p. [3].

Crandall 2936.

Other editions: New Orleans: Printed at the Daily Delta Job Office, 1861. 12 p. 22 cm. (Not in Crandall or Harwell); Richmond: Chas. H. Wynne, Printer, 1862. 15 p. 22 cm. (Crandall 2937).

Maryland, my Maryland, and There's life in the old land yet, by
J. R. Randall, late of Baltimore. Respectfully dedicated to the
Army of the Potomac, by the ladies of Richmond. Richmond:
Printed by Macfarland ₍sic₎ and Ferguson ₍sic₎, 1862.
8 p. 16.5 cm.

"It ₍'There's Life in the Old Land Yet'₎ soon . . . went home to the
hearts of the expatriated Marylanders, who in Virginia are fighting
against the despotism which crushes their fatherland; and, indeed,
throughout the Army of the Potomac it has been adopted as a favorite
war song, as we learn from several army correspondents of the press. The
correspondent of the Charleston Mercury, writing from Centreville, thus
speaks of the part it was made to play in the ceremony of distributing the
new battle flag to the various regiments of the army: "'All of the officers,
on receiving the "Southern Cross" made their acknowledgments in patriotic pledges to do their duty. The bands then played the familiar air
from Il ₍sic₎ Puritani, to which music some soul stirring lines, suggestive
of the rescue of Maryland, had been written by J. R. Randall, a young
poet of New Orleans, whose fugitive verses have already attracted much
attention.—Printed copies of these verses were distributed among the
several regiments.'"—p. ₍3₎-4.
Crandall 3151.

REA, D. B.   75

Sketches from Hampton's cavalry; embracing the principal exploits of the cavalry in the campaigns of 1862 and 1863. By D. B.
Rea . . . Columbia, S. C.: South Carolinian Steam Press, 1864.
158 p. 22 cm.

Quotation in title: *Quorum magna pars fui.*
Crandall 2658.

₍REID, SAMUEL CHESTER₎ 1818-1897   76

A full account of the capture and wonderful escape of Gen. John
H. Morgan, with Captain T. Henry Hines. Thrilling and interesting incidents. By 290. Atlanta, Georgia: Intelligencer Steam
Power Presses, 1864.
16 p. 22 cm.

Cover-title adds: "Price, 100."

Reprinted from the Atlanta *Intelligencer*, January 8, 1864.

"We publish this morning a full account of Morgan's expedition across the Ohio river, during July last, with the particulars of his wonderful escape from the Ohio Penitentiary, furnished by our talented and enterprising correspondent, 290.

"It will be found full of interest, and as entertaining as a tale of the Arabian Nights. It is the most heroic adventure of the age, and the coolness, bravery, and inventive genius of Capt. Henry Hines, who planned Morgan's escape, stamp him as no ordinary man.

"The account has been copy-righted, and will be issued this week in pamphlet form."—Atlanta *Intelligencer*, January 8, 1864.

Crandall 2659.

RICE, JOHN H. 77

A system of modern geography, compiled from various sources and adapted to the present condition of the world; expressly for the use of schools and academies in the Confederate States of America. In which the political and physical condition of the states comprising the Confederate States of America are fully treated of, and their progress in commerce, education, agriculture, internal improvements and mechanic arts, prominently set forth. By John H. Rice, 1862. Atlanta, Georgia: Franklin Printing House. Wood, Hanleiter, Rice & Co., 1862 [c. 1861].

91 p. 28.5 cm.

At head of cover-title: A new descriptive geography.

Preface dated: Atlanta, March 15th, 1862.

"There were thirteen States originally, when England acknowledged the independence of the United States; they increased to 34. This number was reduced to 20 States, in 1861, by the secession of 14 of the Southern States, which formed a new Government under the title of the Confederate States of America, upon a permanent basis, the corner stone of which is African Slavery—which has shorn the United States of nearly all its greatness and prosperity. This secession was caused by the gross injustice of the Northern States in repeated oppressive violations of the Constitution."—p. 51.

"This book supplies an actual necessity in the Confederacy. It is important, in the first place, as giving a fair and impartial account of our country, both as a nation, and of the different states which compose that nation. It is the first Geography to recognize our claims to nationality, and the only one to do us justice independently of nationality. . . .

"Instead of this Geography being full of anti-slavery paragraphs, it is full of pro-slavery passages, and thus commends itself to Southern people.

". . . If we do not encourage our own—if we do not band together for our own protection, how long will it be, after peace is made, before Yankee literature, gotten up chiefly by pauper labor and pauper brains, will flood our country, to the exclusion of the issues from our own press? We believe that this should be prohibited by law. We believe that Yankee literature should be excluded from the Confederacy by statute, after the war is ended. Thanks to the despicable old Gorilla for keeping it out now.

"The book before us is open to criticism in some of its details. This fact, however, does not interfere with its general excellence as a school book. We think that no teacher who does not use it, or some other Southern Geography, if there be another, should be allowed any pay from the public school fund. There should be a provision of law to this effect." *The Countryman*, I, no. 11 (May 13, 1862), p. ₍2₎.

Crandall 4077.

SEMMES, RAPHAEL, 1809-1877   78

> The cruise of the Alabama and the Sumter, from the private journals and other papers of Commander R. Semmes, C. S. N., and other officers. London: Saunders, Otley and Co.; Richmond, Va.: West and Johnson ₍sic₎, 1864.
> xii, 338 p. 18.5 cm.

Harrild, printer, London.
Cover-title omits Richmond imprint.
Engraving of the *Alabama* in cover-title.
"Captain Semmes' diary will delight his friends and all those who can admire the display of those qualities which are necessary for carrying out a difficult and hazardous enterprise. In the management of his crew Captain Semmes displayed tact and vigour, and we know how devoted his men were to him in spite of what may appear to the unprofessional reader very severe discipline. We suppose that never before did a commander so frankly set forth all the troubles and anxieties that are incident to keeping a ship's crew in order."— *The Index* (London), IV (1864), 507.

Harwell 1040.

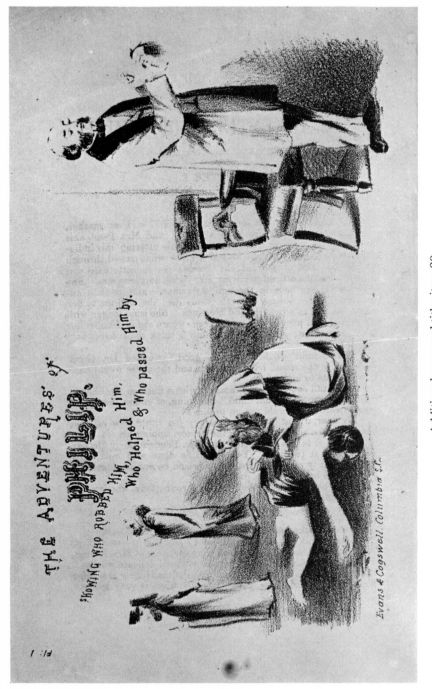

Additional engraved title, item 90.

XXIV.

ADDRESSES OF HON. DANIEL W. VOORHEES, of Indiana; comprising his Argument delivered at Charlestown, Va., Nov. 8, 1859, upon the Trial of JOHN E. COOK, for Treason and Murder; also, an Address delivered before the Literary Societies of the University of Virginia, July 4, 1860.
　　　　　　　　　　　　　　　　　　　　　Price, 50c.

☞ Two noble productions, which will ever hold their place among the splendid efforts of American forensic power.

XXV.

CHIEF POINTS IN THE LAWS OF WAR AND NEUTRALITY, SEARCH AND BLOCKADE. With the changes of 1863 and those now proposed. By JOHN FRASER MACQUEEN, ESQ., one of her Majesty's Counsel.
　　　　　　　　　　　　　　　　　　　　　Price, $1 50.

☞ This admirable little Work is from the pen of an able and learned British Jurist, already well known by his many Works of the highest authority among the legal profession. The present production is of great interest and research, and should be in the hands of every statesman and scholar.

XXVI.

RESOURCES OF THE SOUTHERN FIELDS AND FORESTS, Medical, Economical and Agricultural: Being also a Medical Botany of the Confederate States; with Practical Information on the Useful Properties of the Trees, Plants and Shrubs. By FRANCIS PEYRE PORCHER, Surgeon P. A. C. S. 1 vol., 8vo., ½ Morocco, pp. 601.　　Price, $10

☞ This is, in reality, one of the most splendidly useful Books ever printed in America. What Audubon did for our Ornithology, that Dr. Porcher has done for our Vegetable Kingdom. His is, indeed, a great Work, and no chemist, farmer, doctor or educated gentlemen, who would know the graces of God to this favored Confederacy, can well dispense with it.

XXVII.

PRESCIENCE; A SPEECH delivered by Hon. BEVERLY TUCKER, of Virginia, in the Southern Convention held at Nashville, Tenn., April 18, 1850.　　　　Price, 25c.

☞ That which is good, scholarly and statesmanlike in politics, should never be permitted to perish. That this manly and noble speech, so singularly prophetic is almost all of its theres, possesses, to an eminent degree, these characteristics, it is not feared that the candid reader will question. It contains the thoughts of a Seer, robed in the elegant diction of a scholar, bravely and fearlessly uttered.

XXVIII.

A CONTROVERSY between "ERSKINE" and "W. M." on the Practicability of Suppressing Gambling.　Price, 50c.

XXIX.

THE SECOND BATTLE OF MANASSAS; With Sketches of the (then) Recent Campaigns in Northern Virginia and on the Upper Potomac. Prepared from Special Materials. By the Author of "The First Year of the War."

XXX.

THE SEVEN DAYS BATTLES BEFORE RICH-MOND, &c., &c. By THE SAME.

☞ A very graphic description, by a talented writer, and a necessary companion to his popular History.

XXXI.

THE PARTISAN LEADER. A Novel; and an Apocalypse of the Origin and Struggles of the Southern Confederacy. By Judge BEVERLY TUCKER, of Virginia. Originally published in 1836, now re-published and edited by Rev. THOS. A. WARE.

☞ "These indefatigable Publishers, West & Johnston, have reproduced another Book, which is having a great run, and, what is better, deserves to have it. 'The Partisan Leader,' that celebrated Work, published by the late Judge Beverly Tucker, in 1836, and which so marvellously applies to current events, that some persons, not acquainted with its origin, have seemed to suspect that it must have been gotten up since the beginning of the present war. It is a thrilling and powerful narrative."—Richmond Dispatch.

XXXII.

THE PICTORIAL PRIMER; Designed for the use of Schools and Families. Embellished with fine Designs of Engraving.　　　　　　　　　　　　　　　　Price, 50c.

☞ An important desideratum supplied for parents and teachers.

XXXIII.

THE MAP OF VIRGINIA.　　　　Price, $4.
　　"　"　NORTH CAROLINA.
　　"　"　SOUTH CAROLINA.
　　"　"　KENTUCKY.
　　"　"　TENNESSEE.

War songs of the South. Edited by "Bohemian," correspondent Richmond Dispatch . . . Richmond, West & Johnston, 1862.
216 p. 18.5 cm.

Virginian Power-Presses Print., C. A. Schaffter, printer, Lynchburg, Virginia.

Quotation on title page: "'I said, I knew a very wise man so much of Sir Chr——'s sentiment, that he believed if a man were permitted to make all the ballads, he need not care who should make the laws of a nation.'—Fletcher's *Political Works,* p. 372."

"Southern independence has struck the lyre as well as unsheathed the sword.

"That it has inspired many a song no less truly political than intensely patriotic, our newspapers amply testify. But the newspapers can give only an ephemeral life to 'thoughts that breathe and words that burn.' The book embalms if it does not immortalize."—"Preface," p. 3.

Crandall 3154.

[SIMMS, WILLIAM GILMORE] 1806-1870   80

Sack and destruction of the city of Columbia, S. C. To which is added a list of the property destroyed. Columbia, S. C.: Power Press of Daily Phoenix, 1865.
76 p. 20.5 cm.

The cover-title adds: Originally published in the Columbia Daily Phoenix.

Poem signed "J. H. H." [John Hill Hewitt] on verso of title page.

Printed on Confederate bond paper.

"Humiliation spreads her ashes over our homes and garments, and the universal wreck exhibits only one common aspect of despair. It is for us, as succinctly as possible, and in the simplest language, to endeavor to make the melancholy record of our wretchedness as complete as possible."—p. [3].

Crandall 2661.

SLAUGHTER, PHILIP   81

. . . A sketch of the life of Randolph Fairfax, a private in the ranks of the Rockbridge Artillery, attached to the "Stonewall Brigade" and subsequently to the 1st Reg. Va. Light Artillery, 2d

Corps, Army of Northern Virginia; including a brief account of Jackson's celebrated valley campaign. By the Rev. Philip Slaughter, editor of the "Army and Navy Messenger." Richmond, Va.: Tyler, Allegre & McDaniel, Enquirer Job Office, 1864.
48 p. 19 cm.

At head of title: ⟨Second edition.⟩
No copy of the first edition has been located.
"This pamphlet is the work of Rev. Philip Slaughter, an eminent divine of the Episcopal Church in Virginia, and is designed to commemorate one of the most splendid illustrations of the Christian hero which the war has exhibited. The sketch seems to have been a labor of love to its distinguished author, and is a fitting tribute to virtues which though unostentatiously displayed in the humble position of private, were yet so conspicuous as to elicit eulogy from the illustrious commander of the Army of Northern Virginia, and the no less honourable testimonials of his brave comrades in arms. We regret that our limited space does not permit the republication of the noble letter of Gen. Lee to the father of the gallant youth, written a few days after his fall at the first battle of Fredericksburg."—*Southern Literary Messenger*, xxxvi (1864), 318.
Crandall 2605.

SMITH, WILLIAM RUSSELL, 1815-1896   82
The history and debates of the Convention of the people of Alabama, begun and held in the city of Montgomery, on the seventh day of January, 1861; in which is preserved the speeches of the secret sessions and many valuable state papers. By William R. Smith, one of the delegates from Tuscaloosa. Montgomery: White, Pfister & Co.; Tuscaloosa: D. Woodruff; Atlanta: Wood, Hanleiter, Rice & Co., 1861.
v p., 1 l., [9]-464, xii p. 22.5 cm.

"Of the Conventions of the People that have recently been held in the seceding States on the great question of dissolving the Union, there does not seem to have been any serious effort made, in any except Alabama, to preserve the Debates. It is, therefore, my agreeable fortune, not only to be able to set an example of diligence to the sister States, but to combine, in an authentic record for future ages, both the acts of the PATRIOTS of Alabama, and the fervent words by which they were mutually animated in the discharge of their great duties."—"Preface," p. ₍iii₎.

Crandall 2845.

₍SMITH, WILLIAM RUSSELL₎ 1815-1896   83

The royal ape: a dramatic poem. Richmond: West & Johnston, 1863.

85 p. 23 cm.

Printed at the South Carolinian Book and Job Office, Columbia, S. C.

"This is a Satirical Drama, full of broad humor and severe irony, directed against Lincoln and Lincolnism. It is in the vein of Aristophanes, and certainly the best production of the kind that has yet appeared in the South."—West & Johnston, *Descriptive Catalogue of Publications* (₍Richmond: 1864₎), p. 16.

"We have received from ₍West & Johnston₎ a copy of a dramatic poem, entitled *'The Royal Ape.'* It is a satire upon the Yankee government, and is not without merit. We cannot recommend this work, however, for it is in some places grossly indecent, and we confess that such spiciness is not what we desire to see in Southern literature. We would not put the book into the hands of a child or a lady. It is gotten up very neatly, and we regret that such an excellent house should have put forth such a book."—*The Magnolia Weekly*, I (1862-63), 232.

Crandall 3231.

SOUTH CAROLINA. Convention, 1860-1862   84

The address of the people of South Carolina assembled in Convention, to the people of the slaveholding states of the United States. Printed by order of the Convention. Charleston: Evans & Cogswell, Printers to the Convention, 1860.

16 p. 24 cm.

Written by Robert Barnwell Rhett and adopted as the report of the committee on relations with the other Southern states.

"On the motion of Mr. Cheves, it was *Resolved*, That fifteen thousand copies be printed of the Address to the Southern States, the Declaration of Causes, and the Report of the Committee on the Address of Members of the General Assembly of Georgia."—South Carolina. Convention, 1860-1862. *Journal of the Convention* (Charleston: 1861), p. 95.

Printed in *The Mercury*, Charleston, December 25, 1860.

Crandall 1865.

Declaration of the immediate causes which induce and justify the secession of South Carolina from the Federal Union; and the Ordinance of Secession. Printed by order of the Convention. Charleston: Evans & Cogswell, Printers to the Convention, 1860. 13 p. 23 cm.

Presented by Christopher G. Memminger as the report of the committee to draw up the declaration.

Two issues of this title are exactly alike except for the following points: The cover-title in one has "cause" instead of "causes," and the imprint of that printing reads on the cover: "Charleston: Evans & Cogswell, Printers to the Convention, No. 3 Broad and 103 East Bay Streets, 1860." The imprint in the cover-title of the other issue reads: "Charleston: Printed by Evans & Cogswell, 3 Broad and 103 East Bay Street, 1860." An additional variant is described in Catalogue 163, *Americana*, of Edward Eberstadt & Sons (New York: 1964), item 189. In this copy the cover-title has both "causes" and "streets" in its wording.

Printed in *The Mercury*, Charleston, December 27, 1860.

Crandall 1873.

Spence, James, 1816-   86

The American union; its effect on national character and policy, with an inquiry into secession as a constitutional right, and the causes of the disruption. By James Spence. First American edition, from the fourth and revised (English) edition. Richmond: West and Johnston, 1863. xxiv, 262 p. 19 cm.

Evans & Cogswell, printers, Charleston, S. C.

"The effect of the Union on the national character and policy is here discussed by a bold English thinker who at the same time institutes an exhausting inquiry as to the constitutional right of secession, which he maintains broadly and unqualifiedly. . . . We commend the book to our readers."—*Southern Literary Messenger*, xxxv (1863), 192.

Crandall 2846.

A statement of twelve citizens ieprisoned [sic] in Huntsville, Alabama. Montgomery, Ala.: Montgoeery [sic] Advertiser Book and Job Office, 1862.   87
20 p. 21.5 cm.

Signed: Wm. McDowell, Wm. Acklen, A. J. Withers, Geo. P. Beirne, Wm. H. Moore, S. Cruse, J. G. Wilson, T. S. McCalley, G. L. Mastin, Stephen W. Harris, Thomas Fearne, Henry C. Lay.

Dated: Huntsville, Ala., Sept. 2d. 1862.

Harwell 1092.

STEPHENS, ALEXANDER HAMILTON, 1812-1883   88

The great speech of Hon. Alex H. Stephens, delivered before the Georgia legislature, on Wednesday night, March 16th, 1864, to which is [sic] added extracts prom [sic] Gov. Brown's message to the Georgia legislature. [Milledgeville: 1864].

32 p. 20.5 cm.

Caption title.

Crandall 2848.

Another edition omits the extracts from Brown's message: Atlanta: Intelligencer Steam Power Presses, 1864. 28 p. 21.5 cm. (Crandall 2849).

... THE STRANGER'S GUIDE and official directory for the city of Richmond, showing the location of the principal buildings and offices of the Confederate, state and city governments, residences of the principal officers, etc. [Richmond:] G. P. Evans & Co., Printers, 1863.   89

Cover-title, 31 p. 16.5 cm.

At head of title: No. 1. October, Vol. 1. Price, 50 cents.

Vignette in title.

No more published.

"The object of this publication is to supply a want which has long been felt, not only by strangers arriving in the city, but by numbers of our citizens. The immense amount of business arising from the prosecution of the war has been distributed among a large number of departments, bureaux, etc., which are located in so many different places that persons having business at some of them are unable to find them except by persistent inquiry. This little book will tell them where the various offices are situated."—"To the Reader," p. 1.

Crandall 2677.

Another edition has the same title but is completely reset and has a different woodcut as the vignette in the title. On it the words at the head of the title are printed: No. 1.⟩ October. ⟨Vol. 1. Price, 50 cts. This issue measures 14.5 cm. (Crandall 2676).

The adventures of Philip on his way through the world; showing
who robbed him, who helped him, and who passed him by. By
W. M. Thackeray. With illustrations. Columbia, S. C.: Evans
and Cogswell, 1864.

vii, [9]-496 p. front. (port.), 12 plates. 18 cm.

"If we could say anything which would add to the circulation of the
novel whose title is quoted above, we would do so. But the name of
Thackeray forms a sufficient passport to ensure the currency of any
work of which he is the author. All that is necessary in this case, is a
bare announcement of the work."—*The Countryman*, XX (1865), 46.

Crandall 3111.

Our danger and our duty; by Rev. J. H. Thornwell. Columbia,
S. C.: Southern Guardian Steam-Power Press, 1862.
14 p. 20.5 cm.

Crandall 2859.

Published also as Tract no. 64 of the Soldiers' Tract Association of
the M. E. Church, South (Richmond: n. d.) 16 p. (Crandall 4892); Tract
no. 130 of the South Carolina Tract Society (Charleston: n. d.) 16 p.
(Crandall 4890); and Tract no. 215 of the Evangelical Tract Society
(Petersburg: 1863) 15 p. (Crandall 4891).

The partisan leader: a novel, and an apocalypse of the origin and
struggles of the Southern Confederacy. By Judge Beverley
Tucker . . . Originally published in 1836. Now re-published and
edited by Rev. Thos. A. Ware. Richmond: West & Johnston,
1862.

viii, 220 p. 23.5 cm.

Macfarlane & Fergusson, printers.

" 'These indefatigable Publishers, West & Johnston, have reproduced
another Book, which is having a great run, and, what is better, deserves
to have it. "The Partisan Leader," that celebrated work, published by
the late Judge Beverl[e]y Tucker, in 1836, and which so marvellously
applies to current events, that some persons, not acquainted with its

origin, have seemed to suppose that it must have been gotten up since the beginning of the present war. It is a thrilling and powerful narrative.' —*Richmond Dispatch.*"—West & Johnston, *Descriptive Catalogue of Publications* (₁Richmond: 1864₁), p. 19.

"'The Partisan Leader' supplies a great *desideratum*. It answers all the requirements of the public taste at this time. Interesting as a novel, surprising as a work of prophecy, and invaluable as an incentive to the prosecution of the existing struggle, and as an assurance of our ultimate success, it cannot fail to meet with universal favor."—*Southern Literary Messenger*, xxxiv (1862), 400.

Crandall 3112.

TUCKER, NATHANIEL BEVERLEY, 1784-1851   93

Prescience. Speech delivered by Hon. Beverl₁e₁y Tucker, of Virginia, in the Southern Convention, held at Nashville, Tenn., April 13th, 1850. Richmond, Va.: West & Johnston, 1862.
38 p. 21 cm.

"That which is good, scholarly, and statesmanlike, in politics, should never be permitted to perish. That the following manly and able speech, so singularly prophetic in almost all of its themes, possess₁es₁, to an eminent degree, these characteristics, it is not feared that the candid reader will question. It contains the thoughts of a Seer, robed in the elegant diction of a scholar, bravely and fearlessly uttered. The publishers feel that they need, at this crisis, offer the public no apology for the republication of such a production; but if such apology were necessary, they might plead the pressing requests to this effect of the numerous friends and admirers of the venerable statesman, the offspring of whose genius it is."—"Publisher's Advertisement," p. ₁iii₁.

"This history of this oration, so like a prophecy, is remarkable. Spoken almost inaudibly, because of the weak and lagging speech of him who uttered it, condemned then as a crazed visionary, revered now as a wondrous seer, it fell still born, in the abortive Southern Convention of 1850. Published at request of the author's friends, it struggled for a hearing through the press; struggled vainly among a people bowing down each to his own false god, shutting their ears to this Jonah, preaching the wrath to come. As the years went round and the end came, first one and then another of those who loved their country, began the more to consider its warnings. And now that thought has become reality, and prophecy more than justified by fact, the discerning public begs to read the prophecy. The able publisher is ready with his type.

"So, after eleven years of deaf neglect—of dullest oblivion—all men praise, who would not read; all men wonder who would but sneer; and no ass is there so dull but brays his coarse approval over the dead prophet's grave. No room for criticism. Have not all-discovering Time, and the clear eyed, oh, wise public, discerned how truly he spoke, how clearly saw? So let us call it Prescience, and say, each to other, I knew it long ago, when he spoke it; the great old man, who moulders now into common clay. And we will smile at this pleasant lie, deceiving none, and go our ways; and when the next prophet comes, sneer at him, decry him, neglect him, till we shout over him and lie about him in his grave as we have over this one.

"Lie as we may, we speak truth when we call this, his death song, great, cogent, not to be shaken in its logic; fierce, clean cutting in its invective; ardent, inspiring in love of country; far-sighted, true in its prophecy. One thing only he could not foresee, the madness that could make this war. But, should it come, truly he saw the result as it is working around us to-day.

"All contained in this oration, Prescience, deserves a place in the memory of the South, and of Virginia; one sentence of it, at least, should be engraved in golden letters, the motto of every Virginian's home:

" 'What Virginia says, I am ever ready to vindicate; what Virginia does, I, at all hazards and to the last extremity, will maintain.' "— *Southern Literary Messenger*, xxxiv (1862), 80.

Crandall 2871.

TYSON, BRYAN   94

A ray of light; or, A treatise on the sectional troubles, religiously and morally considered. By Bryan Tyson. Brower's Mills, N. C.: The Author, 1862.
170 p., 1 l. 19 cm.

"I hereby send you a book, which I hope you will carefully read, and consider well the object for which it was written—to arrest the farther progress of this terrible civil war now upon us, and to speedily bring about a reconciliation between the two sections. I though indulge but a feeble hope that anything I can say upon this all-important subject will be heeded; for, in all probability, this terrible civil war now upon us will, before ended, rage with a much more destructive fury than it has yet done; but, whether or not it avail anything towards bringing about the desired object, I feel that I shall have discharged my duty; that I have done all that I can do towards bringing about a reconciliation between the two sections, and restoring quietude to our now dismembered country."—Broadside by Tyson printed at Brown's ₁*sic*₁ Mills, N. C., dated September 24, 1862, and reprinted in the North (probably in Washington) in 1863 with some additional material at the end.

Crandall 2872.

THE WAR AND ITS HEROES. Illustrated. Richmond: Ayres & Wade, 1864.   95

v, ₁1₁, ₁17₁-88 p. incl. illus., 6 ports. 23 cm.

The cover-title is framed in an elaborate engraving by Hurdle and reads: The war and its heroes, first series, containing portraits and biographies of Generals Cooper, Longstreet, J. E. Johnston, Pemberton, G. W. Smith, Lee, Ewell, Hood, Hindman, Jackson, A. P. Hill, Hampton, Lane, M. L. Smith; Commodore Hollins; and Majors Mosby and Pelham.

No more published.

"The series will consist of four or more volumes. . . . The engravings have been executed with care and skill and are taken from special photographs obtained by the Publishers themselves. The biographical sketches, which accompany them, are made up from official reports and private information from the most reliable sources."—"Preface," p. ₁iii₁.

Crandall 2609.

WARDER, T. B.   96

Battle of Young's Branch; or, Manassas Plain, fought July 21, 1861. With maps of the battle field made by actual survey, and the various positions of the regiments and artillery companies placed thereon, with an account of the movements of each, procured from the commanding officer, or an officer of the regiment. Also, an account of the battle. Also, the battle ground of the 18th July, 1861, with General Beauregard's report of said battle. By T. B. Warder & Jas. M. Catlett. Richmond: Enquirer Book and Job Press, Tyler, Wise, Allegre and Smith, 1862.

2 p. l., ₁7₁-156 p., 1 l. maps. 15.5 cm.

The maps were drawn by John Grant and lithographed by Hoyer & Ludwig, Richmond, for inclusion in the official report of the battle.

"It is designed to give the movements of the two armies in this great battle with such accuracy as to enable the professional reader to derive the instruction concerning the management of troops when engaged in battle that could not be gained otherwise except upon the battle field; and to become acquainted with the manoeuvrings necessary to ensure success."—"Preface," p. ₍5₎.

Crandall 2662.

[WEST, BECKWITH]   97

Experience of a Confederate States prisoner, being an ephemeris regularly kept by an officer of the Confederate States Army. Richmond: West & Johnston, Publishers, 1862.
64 p. 21.5 cm.

At lower left of title page (below imprint): ₍rule₎ | G. W. Gary, Printer.

"The gallant Morgan has said that our independence is an achieved fact. 'Privation and suffering have won it.' It is true that the noble South has been deprived of many of its wonted necessaries, not to say luxuries, by the present invasion of those disciples of Satan, commonly called 'Yankees.' Paper, among other things, is scarce in the South, and paper may be turned into excellent account in the composition of cartridges, while metal that might be moulded into bullets is run into type. Yet newspapers and books are printed, and most of them eagerly read, especially any that have the most remote bearing upon the present contest. In these stern times of war's realities, plain facts challenge our attention rather than the gaudy fiction of novels. Honey from Mount Hybla, or Nectar from Olympus, would fail on the palate unless relieved by homelier viands; and it would certainly require considerable stoicism to sit down to a tale of imaginary woes and sorrows while one great wail is going up from our sick and wounded—an incredible amount of apathy to sit leisurely down to such a book under the shade of a tree while the nation is sending out a heartcry for reinforcements to our brave legions, in order to *speedily* defeat the unscrupulous enemy. This little book is intended as, and professes no more than a plain statement of facts, so that others may learn what I have read, seen and heard, without undergoing the pain of incarceration in the hands of Yankees, whose tyranny increases in proportion to the power they possess over their victims."—"Preface," p. ₍3₎.

Crandall 2664.

[56]

Descriptive catalogue of publications issued by West & Johnston, Richmond. ₁Richmond: West & Johnston₁ C. H. Wynne, Printer ₁1864₁.
Cover-title, 24 p. 23 cm.

Caption title: Catalogue of new and important publications, published by West & Johnston, 145 Main street, Richmond.

Lists seventy-six titles, plus nine "In the press." Includes a few titles published before secession and a few issued by other publishers but for sale by West & Johnston.

Crandall 3289.

₁WILSON, AUGUSTA JANE (EVANS)₁ 1835-1909   99

Macaria; or, Altars of sacrifice. By the author of "Beulah" . . . Richmond: West & Johnston, 1864.
183 p. 23.5 cm.

Evans & Cogswell, printers, Columbia, S. C.

"That Macaria is a great novel, I will not pretend to deny; but that it is not at all comparable with Beulah, every candid reader will admit. Macaria will never be a popular novel, for the reason that the mass of readers will not understand her classical allusions . . . If Miss Evans is not actually pedantic, she is certainly obscure."—Joel Chandler Harris in *The Countryman*, xx (1865), 42-43.

"We are convinced of its great superiority to any similar production of Southern writers during the war, and are pleased to note its appearance as the most promising indication we have yet seen of a future elevated standard of Fiction among Southern Authors."—*Southern Literary Messenger*, xxxvi (1864), 317.

"The South surpasses the North not only in chivalry and military genius, but in the high civilization of surpassing literature also. Macaria is the product of a female mind, but masculine, learned and grand, beyond the qualities usually found among literateurs of that sex. It is at once honorable to the South and hopeful of its future."—The London *Times*, quoted in advertisement of West & Johnston in the *Daily Richmond Examiner*, October 26, 1864.

". . . In 'Macaria,' the authoress of 'Beulah' has depended too much on her scrap-book, and too little upon her own rich imagination. We sincerely trust that with 'Macaria' that scrap-book is entirely exhausted, and that when next we meet her in the walks of literature, she will have learned to eschew the tinkling of borrowed trinkets, and founded for herself a taste and style based upon no less an idea than that of Intellectual Independence."—*The Southern Illustrated News*, III (1864), 148.

Crandall 3114.

There were two editions of ten thousand copies each. The second edition is so noted on the title page and has the date on the cover changed to 1865 (Crandall 3115).

YANCEY, WILLIAM LOWNDES, 1814-1863   100

Speeches of William L. Yancey, Senator from the State of Alabama; made in the Senate of the Confederate States during the session commencing on the eighteenth day of August, A. D. 1862. Montgomery, Ala.: Montgomery Advertiser Book and Job Office, 1862.

54 p.   21.5 cm.

Crandall 2879.